Alfred John Church

With the King at Oxford

A tale of the Great Rebellion

Alfred John Church

With the King at Oxford
A tale of the Great Rebellion

ISBN/EAN: 9783337174200

Printed in Europe, USA, Canada, Australia, Japan

Cover: Foto ©ninafisch / pixelio.de

More available books at **www.hansebooks.com**

With the KING at OXFORD

A TALE OF THE GREAT REBELLION

BY THE

Rev. Alfred J. Church, M.A.

Professor of Latin in University College, London
Author of "Stories from Homer"

With Sixteen Illustrations

LONDON
SEELEY & CO., 46, 47 & 48, ESSEX STREET, STRAND
(LATE OF 54, FLEET STREET)
1886.
All Rights Reserved

TO

George William Fleetwood Bury,

PHYSICIAN AND FRIEND,

THIS BOOK IS DEDICATED.

I cannot allow this book to appear without the expression of my thanks to the Rev. Andrew Clark, Fellow of Lincoln College, Oxford, who very kindly put at my service a number of interesting records of the domestic history of the College.

A. C.

HADLEY GREEN,
October, 1885.

CONTENTS

CHAP.		PAGE
I.	OF MY BIRTH AND BRINGING-UP	1
II.	OF MY SOJOURN IN LONDON	13
III.	OF THE PLAGUE AND OTHER MATTERS	26
IV.	OF THINGS AT HOME	40
V.	OF THINGS AT OXFORD	52
VI.	OF THE KING'S GOING TO WORCESTER	65
VII.	OF THE FIGHT AT COPREDY BRIDGE	81
VIII.	OF THE PLAGUE AT OXFORD AND OTHER MATTERS	93
IX.	BEFORE NASEBY	105
X.	OF NASEBY FIGHT	120
XI.	AFTER NASEBY	131
XII.	OF MY FATHER'S END AND OTHER MATTERS	152
XIII.	OF MY COMING BACK TO OXFORD	174
XIV.	OF BODLEY'S LIBRARY	185
XV.	OF THE VISITORS AT OXFORD	197
XVI.	OF MY KINSFOLK AT ENSTONE	209
XVII.	OF MY GOING TO LONDON	224
XVIII.	OF THE TRIAL OF THE KING	238
XIX.	OF THE KING'S DEATH	252
XX.	OF MATTERS AT ENSTONE	263
XXI.	OF MY ADVENTURES AT SEA	275
	EPILOGUE	293

LIST OF ILLUSTRATIONS

	PAGE
A MUSKETEER	*Frontispiece*
LONDON BRIDGE	14
FRIAR BACON'S HOUSE	70
KING CHARLES THE FIRST	72
HALT OF OFFICERS	76
A GUNNER	88
MERTON COLLEGE, OXFORD	96
A CAVALRY SKIRMISH	122
A PIKEMAN	126
GATEWAY OF CHRISTCHURCH, OXFORD . . .	176
THE LAST ABBOT OF OSENEY	178
THE BODLEIAN LIBRARY, OXFORD	190
PORCH OF ST. MARY'S, OXFORD	202
VICE-CHANCELLOR AND ESQUIRE BEDELLS . . .	204
THE TRIAL OF KING CHARLES . .	248
THE EXECUTION OF THE KING . . .	260

With the KING at OXFORD

CHAPTER I.

OF MY BIRTH AND BRINGING-UP.

My father was the son of a gentleman of Oxfordshire that had a small estate near to the town of Eynsham, in that county. The monks of Eynsham Priory had the land aforetime; and 'twas said that here, as elsewhere, there was a curse upon such as held for their own uses that which had been dedicated to God's service. How this may be I know not, though there are notable instances—as, to wit, the Russells—in which no visible curse has fallen on the holders of such goods; but it is certain that my father's forbears wasted their estate grievously. Being but the third son, he had scarce, in any case, tarried at home; but, matters being as they were, the emptiness of the family purse drove him out betimes into the world. Being of good birth and breeding he got, without much ado, a place about the Court, which was not, however, much to his liking. I have heard him say—and this, though, as will be seen hereafter, he was a great lover of monarchy—that, between a weak king and villainous courtiers, Whitehall was no place for an honest gentleman. Robert Carr, that was afterwards Earl of Somerset, he liked little, and George Villiers, Duke of Buckingham, he liked yet less, being, as he was wont to say, by so much a greater villain than Somerset as a duke is greater than an earl. He was right glad, therefore, to leave the "sunshine of the Royal presence;" for so did men speak of the Court in the hyperbolical language of those times, even for so dismal and outlandish a part as Ireland. But I know not whether he did not wish himself back, for of Ireland he would never afterwards speak with any measure of patience, declaring that he knew not which were the worse, the greediness and cruelty of the

English conquerors, or the savagery and unreason of the native people. Here he tarried for some three or four years, having, indeed, had bestowed upon him an estate, which, for its boundaries, at least, was of considerable magnitude, but from which he received nothing but trouble. Who hath it now I know not; and, indeed, he charged me to have nought to do with it, saying—for I remember his very words—"If they will give thee the whole island in fee, say them nay, for it is fit for nothing but to be drowned under the sea." Yet his next venture was not one whit happier, as will be readily concluded, when I say that he took service with Sir Walter Raleigh, whom he chanced to fall in with at Cork, at which place Sir Walter touched on his way to the Indies in search of gold. Gold got they none, but of hard blows not a few, and of pains and sickness still more. My father was with the boats that sailed up the river Orinoco, and caught in his arms, I have heard him say, Walter Raleigh the younger, when this last was slain by a bullet from a Spanish arquebuse. From this voyage he came back beggared in and purse not a little broken in health; to the end of his days indeed he suffered much at times from the fever that he contracted in those parts. The year following that wherein Raleigh was beheaded, came what seemed at the first sight good news, namely, that the Bohemians had bestowed the crown of their country upon the Elector of Bavaria, husband to the Princess Elizabeth, the king's daughter. Thereupon there arose such a tumult of joy throughout the country as the oldest man living scarce remembered to have heard before. There was nothing too good to be hoped for as about to come from this promotion. Indeed, I have heard my father say that he was himself present when the Archbishop of Canterbury (Dr. Abbott) preached a sermon wherein he declared that this event was foretold in Scripture, naming even the chapter and verse, which were, if I remember right, in the Book of the Revelation. My father was carried away with the rest, and having, as may well be thought, a special gift for choosing for his own that which should be the losing side, forthwith took service with the Elector, to whom King James, though scarce approving of the cause, sent at this time auxiliaries to the number of four thousand. In this army my father had a captain's commission, with pay to the amount of four shillings by the day—handsome wages, only that he never received of them so much as a doit. Nor did the campaign recompense the defect of gains by any excess of glory. It was, indeed, as barren of laurels as of gold ; and my father, who, being favourably known of old time by the Princess, was appointed to command the guard of the Elector, arrived in his Highness's company at the Hague without a penny in his pocket, and scarce a coat to his back.

But now behold a turn of Fortune's wheel. While he lingered in Holland, not from choice, indeed, but from compulsion, seeing that he did not possess the wherewithal to pay his passage to England, came news of an inheritance that had fallen to him, being nothing less—or, may be, I should rather say, considering its poverty, nothing more—than the family estate. This fell to my father by the death of his two elder brothers, who both expired of a fever on the same day. And this day, so strangely do things fall together in this world, was the very same as that on which all his worldly hopes seemed to have been overset, that is, the 8th of November, in the year 1620, when the Elector Palatine was utterly defeated by the Duke of Bohemia. My father then, coming, as I have said, to Holland this same winter with the Elector, there heard of his inheritance, not, indeed, without some natural regret for the cause that had brought it to him, yet, because his brothers were older by far, and akin by half-blood only, and strangers by long interruption of acquaintance, not sorrowful overmuch.

The said inheritance was, as may be gathered from what has been written above, a mighty poor thing, being, after all debts and encumbrances were paid, but of sixty pounds value by the year at the most. Nevertheless, for a poor, battered soldier that had no way to earn his bread, 'twas by no means to be despised. Veterans that have passed through the wars— if my father, that was but just thirty years of age, may be so called—do commonly love the quietude of a country retreat (and it was thus that Augustus Cæsar and others did reward

OF MY BIRTH AND BRINGING-UP.

their legions); and my father affected this manner of life as readily as did ever old soldier in the world, and, being a man of useful parts, he turned his sword into a ploughshare with good result, and this not only of profit of money, but of health also. Being thus set up, both in body and estate, he took courage to ask in marriage a maiden of those parts, Cicely Harland by name. She was the daughter of a gentleman that had a like estate with my father, only it was without encumbrance, so that Mistress Cicely was not ill-provided with a portion. My father, whose name—for this I have not yet mentioned—was Philip Dashwood, married Mistress Cicely Harland in the month of September, 1623. Of this marriage were born two children; first, my sister Dorothy, in August, 1624, and secondly myself, a Philip also, who came into this troublesome world on Christmas Day, 1625, having as my birthright, as the gossips say, the gift of seeing spirits, though this I have nèver yet, to my knowledge, enjoyed. My first teaching, save the very rudiments which my dear mother did impart to me, was from Master William Hearnden, parson of the parish, to which, indeed, he had been presented by my father in the vacancy before described. They had been close friends in that luckless campaigning in Bohemia, where Master Hearnden was chaplain to the English regiment—ay, and on occasion also, I have heard say, captain also; for he was, as the country folk say, "a man of his hands." Not the less was he a virtuous and godly clerk, and a sound scholar also, and with a rare gift which scholars, be they ever so sound, have not always—of teaching that which he knew.

On January the 6th, 1633, being then twelve days past my eighth birthday, I was entered of the Merchant Taylors' School, at Laurence Pountney, in the City of London, by the presentation of William Harford, kinsman to my mother, that was one of the Court of the said Company. Mr. Edwards was then master of the school, and remained so during the time of my continuance there.

At the first I lodged in the house of Master William Rushworth, that was a merchant of timber, and dwelt in the Strand, of whom and of whose house more hereafter.

Within a few weeks of my coming I saw what my elders told me was the finest spectacle that had been seen in London within the memory of man, that is, a mighty grand masquerade, with which the gentlemen of the four Inns of Court entertained their Majesties King Charles, and Henrietta of France, his Queen. I was yet too much of a child to have any clear understanding of what I saw, though the number of men and horses, the splendour of scarlet and purple, of gold and silver, and all the magnificence of the show made a notable mark on my mind. But I heard much talk about it in after times; and, indeed, till the late troubles came upon the country, there was nothing of which there was more frequent mention than of this same masquerade. Thus it came to pass that, filling up what I observed at the time with that which I heard afterwards, I came to have such a notion of the matter as might have been conceived by one much older than I then was. If, therefore, I may join together what was afterwards told to me with what I remember of myself, this masquerade was shown on Candlemas Day, which is the second day of February, the procession starting from Chancery Lane when it was now dusk. First came twenty footmen in scarlet liveries, with silver lace, each carrying a torch. These were the Marshal's men that cleared the way, and with them came the Marshal himself, an extraordinary proper handsome gentleman, riding one of the King's horses, with two lackeys, each carrying a torch, and a page that bare his cloak. After these came a hundred gentlemen, five and twenty from each Inn of Court, riding on horses, the finest that could be found in London, and apparelled as bravely as men could be. After these again came what was styled the anti-masque, cripples and beggars on horseback, mounted on the poorest, leanest jades that could be gotten out of the dirt-carts and elsewhere. These had their proper music of keys and tongs, making the queerest noise that can be imagined, but yet with a sort of concert. Then followed another antimasque, this time of birds. The first portion was men on horseback, playing on pipes and whistles, and other instruments by which the notes of birds may be imitated; the second was the birds them-

OF MY BIRTH AND BRINGING-UP.

selves, among which I specially noted an owl in an ivy bush. What these creatures were I knew not at the time, but learnt afterwards that they were little boys put into covers of the shapes of the birds. After these came that which pleased the people mightily, and at which I laughed heartily myself, though not knowing why: this was a satire on the projectors and monopolisers from whom the realm had long suffered. First there was a man riding on a very mean steed that had a great bit in his mouth; and on the man's head was a bit, with reins and headstall fastened to it, and a petition written for a patent that no one in the kingdom should ride their horses save with such bits as they might buy of him. Second to him was another with a bunch of carrots on his head and a capon in his fist, and he had a petition also for a patent, that none should fatten capons save with carrots and by his licence. Behind these came other horsemen, and last of all four chariots, one for each Inn of Court, these being the most splendid of all. The King and Queen were so mightily pleased with this pageant that they desired to see it again. Thereupon the Lord Mayor invited their Majesties to a banquet in the Merchant Taylors' Hall, and the same masque was there again performed, the procession having gone eastward this time. And we scholars of the school were privileged to see it from a gallery that was set apart for us.

CHAPTER II.

OF MY SOJOURN IN LONDON.

My sojourn with Master Rushworth was but for a time. Accordingly some three days, or thereabouts, after that I had been a spectator of the lawyers' great masque, I changed my abode to the house of one Mr. Timothy Drake, a woollen draper, that dwelt upon London Bridge, on the north side. Master Drake was bound to my kinsman Master Harford, of whom I have before spoken, by many obligations of benefits received; and when the said uncle, being single and well advanced in years, was unwilling to be troubled with the charge of a child, Master Drake gladly received me; not, I suppose, without good consideration given. It was judged to be more convenient for me to lodge upon the bridge, which is but little more than a stone's throw from the Merchant Taylors' School, than in the Strand; nor was I unwilling to go, but my sojourn there was but for a very short time, as I shall presently show.

'Twas a marvellous place this same London Bridge, more like, indeed, to a village than a bridge, having on either side houses, some of them being shops, as was that in which I dwelt, and some taverns, and some private dwellings. And about the middle of the bridge stood a great building, which they called Nonesuch House, very splendidly painted with colours, and having wooden galleries hanging over the river, richly ornamented with carving and gilding. This Nonesuch House covered the whole breadth of the bridge from the one side to the other; and in the middle of it was an arch with the road passing under it.

The bridge had, or, I should rather say, has (for it still stands and will, I doubt not, stand for many ages to come) twenty arches, of which one is blocked. They are but small, the purpose of the builder, Peter of Colechurch, having been, it is said, thus to restrain the ebbing of the tide, and so to make the river above the bridge more easily navigable. I should rather think, if I may say so much

London Bridge.

without wrong to the pious man, that in that rude age (now near upon five centuries since) he knew not how to build bigger. And being thus small they are still further diminished by the sterlings that are built about the piers, to keep them from damage by ice or floods. Thus it came to pass that of nine hundred feet (for such is the length of the bridge from end to end) scarce two hundred remain for the waterway. The consequence thereof is that when the water is lower than the sterlings it rushes through the arches with a singular great violence. How great it is may be judged from this, that in some of the arches there is a waterfall, so to speak, of as much as two feet, when the tide is at its strongest; and this strongest is when it is about half-spent, running upwards; but why the flow should be stronger than the ebb I know not, seeing that this latter is increased by the natural current of the river. I do remember, if I may delay those that shall read this chronicle with such childish recollections, how I marvelled at the first at this same ebb and flow, of which I had never before heard. On the first day of my coming to

Master Drake's house, being, as I remember, the seventh day of February, I looked out from my chamber window about half-past five of the clock, and saw the Thames full to his banks and flowing eastward, as by rights he should, it being then but just past the flood. But the next time that I chanced to cast my eyes on him, the tide having but newly begun to flow, lo! he was dwindled to half his span, and ran westward. Of a truth I thought that there was witchcraft, and, being a simple child, ran down into my host's parlour, crying, "What ails the river that it is half-spent and runs the wrong way?" and was much laughed at for my pains.

I thought to have much pleasure from sojourn in the house upon the bridge, and doubtless should have had but for the sad mishap of which I shall shortly speak. For indeed there was much to be seen daily upon the river. On the eastern side, looking, that is to say, towards the sea, there were goodly ships from all parts of the world, lading and unlading their cargoes, for through the bridge none could go; nay, the very wherries, for the violence of the water, would not venture the passage save at the highest or lowest of the tide; but passengers were discharged on the one side and took boat again on the other. And on the western side there were the barges of my Lord Mayor and of the richer of the Companies; and barges of trade, carrying all manner of goods and especially timber, both for building and burning; and small boats almost without number, both of private persons and of watermen that plied for hire. And on occasions there were races among the watermen and also among the 'prentices of the City. And there were other sports, notably that of tilting upon the water, in which the vanquisher would dismount the vanquished, not indeed from his horse but from his boat, and sometimes drive him into the water, with no small laughter from the spectators. The bridge also afforded another pastime, for when the tide was so far ebbed that it was possible to stand upon the sterlings (which were at other times covered with water) there were many fishes to be caught, for these commonly resort where there is abundance of food to be found, as must needs be in so great a city as London. And if any cannot conceive of the anglers' craft as practised in the midst of such din and tumult, they may take as a proof that the makers of anglers' tackle congregate in Crooked Lane, which is hard by the bridge, more than in any other place in London.

Being also a lad, for all my tender years, of an active fancy and apt to muse by myself, and to build castles in the air, or, as some say, in Spain, for my delight, I did not forget the story of Edward Osborne, that was 'prentice to Sir William Hewet, clothworker, some time Lord Mayor of London, how he leapt from the window of one of the bridge houses, and saved his master's daughter that had been dropped into the river by a careless maid. All the dwellers on the bridge have the story ready, so to speak, on the tip of their tongues, as if it were a credit to themselves; nor would I discourage the thought, for haply it might give a lad boldness to venture his life in the like gallant way. Hence, before I had been in the house an hour they showed me the window from which the said Edward leapt. All the world knows, I suppose, how he afterwards married this same daughter, and received with her a great estate, and how he rose to great prosperity, being Lord Mayor in the year 1583, and how his posterity are to this day persons of great worship and renown, who will yet, if I mistake not, rise higher in the state. 'Tis true I was no 'prentice, nor had Master Drake a daughter, save one that must have been forty years of age at the very least; but what are these hindrances to the fancy when it is minded to disport in its own realms?

But now for the mishap which scattered these fancies and the hopes of other delights, of which I have before spoken. I came, as I have said, to sojourn with Master Drake on the seventh day of February, being, as I remember, a Thursday; and on the Monday following my sojourn was ended. Near to Master Drake's house dwelt Mr. John Briggs, a needle-maker by trade, who was wont to keep up a brisk fire for the carrying on of his craft. This being maintained at a greater height and for a longer time together than was customary, trade being beyond ordinary brisk, heated the woodwork adjoining, than which there is, as I conceive, no more common cause of such mischief. This at least, was conjectured at the time, for nothing could be known of a certainty. What is established is, that about ten of the clock at night on Monday aforesaid, the fire began in Mr. Briggs' house, and that so suddenly and with such violence that he and his wife and child, a maid of about four years (who, as being of a more convenient age and size than Mistress Tabitha Drake, I had resolved should fall into the river and be saved by me) escaped with their lives very hardly, having nothing on but their shirts, and it may be said, the smoke, so near did they come to being burned. Nor were we in much better case, save that Master Drake and his wife and daughter, having entertained the parson of the parish to supper ('twas in the parish of St. Magnus the Martyr) had not yet gone to bed. Thus they were able not only to save themselves and me, who was in bed and sound asleep, more easily, but also to carry off some of their chief possessions. As for putting out of the fire, little or nothing could be done. A man might have thought that, the houses being on a bridge, there would be sufficient water at hand to prevent a fire, how great soever. But it was not so. By ill-luck it happened that the river was at its very lowest, so that the engines, of which there were three, newly made, and much admired for their excellence, could get no water from it, and, indeed, were broken in the endeavour. And when the conduits were opened, and the pipes that carried water through the streets cut, these also yielded but little water, so that the fire raged almost without let or hindrance. Yet such water as there was, was used to the uttermost, men carrying the buckets up ladders, which were set against the burning houses, and pouring them upon the flames. From this, indeed, came other damages, for the ladders were burnt through, to the hurt of many, by the breaking of their arms and legs, and even to the loss of their lives. All that night and the next day until noon the fire continued to burn fiercely; nor did it stop till it came to the first empty space upon the bridge; there it was stayed for want of matter, the brewers' men that were on the other side of the river also helping by bringing abundance of water on their drays and wetting the houses that were yet unconsumed. There were forty-three houses burned in all, being about the third part of those that stood upon the bridge. The road was so blocked by the ruins that, though as many as had space to stand laboured to carry away the timber and bricks, and tiles and rubbish, none could pass over the bridge before Wednesday, and there were remains of the fire yet smouldering on the Tuesday following, as I learned to my cost, having on that day burnt my finger with a live coal of fire which I took up in my hand.

By God's mercy, the night was warm, or else the inhabitants that were ousted so suddenly from their homes had suffered much. It was still, also, a matter for which we are yet more bound to be thankful; for had the wind, which was, indeed, from the south, and so blew towards the City, been strong, London itself would have been much endangered, the more so as the traders in Thames Street have much pitch, tar, rosin, oil, and other inflammable goods in their houses. Indeed, were I minded to prophesy, I should say that some day, there will arise in this very part of London, for nowhere is the peril greater, such a conflagration as has never been seen in the world; save only, it may be, when Rome was set on fire by that mad Cæsar, Nero.

As for myself, I found shelter, for the time, with my kinsman, Master Harford, in his fine mansion, hard by the Church of Saint Peter on Cornhill. Whether he would have kept me now that his scheme of lodging me with Master Drake had fallen through, I cannot say; but, if he ever entertained any such purpose, it was shortly dismissed by reason of my behaviour. 'Twas, as I have said, a fine mansion, Master Harford being one of the wealthiest merchants in London, and the table kept proportionate thereto. There was no mistress of the house, Master Harford being, as I have said, a bachelor, but a housekeeper, Joan Fuller by name, a kind woman, and knowing in all the knowledge of the store-room and kitchen, but otherwise of scant sense. She, having none on whom to bestow her affections, save a cat and a dog, took a mighty favour to me, which favour she showed in the fashion that she herself would have most approved, if I may say so much without unkindness to the memory of one that is now deceased; for she plied me, both in season and out of season, with all manner of dainty meats, so that in the space of eight days or thereabouts I fell sick. 'Twas no great matter, only a sickness as would come to any child that had been so dealt with, and was easily set right by the apothecary's medicines, which, to my mind, so nauseous were they, did more than outweigh all the pleasure of my dainty feeding; but it settled Master Harford in his intention to lodge me elsewhere than in his own house. Master Drake could not entertain me any more, having to be content with scant lodging for himself and his wife and daughter. Nor was there any talk of building up the houses again; and this, indeed, was not done for more than thirteen years after the burning; but the sides of the bridge where they had been were covered in with boarding. So it came about that I was sent back to my first lodging with Master Rushworth, in the Strand.

He was, as I have said, a merchant of timber, and had his house in the Strand, on the north side, with a yard on the other side of the street, in which he stored his goods and did his buying and selling. In this I was free to play as much as suited my liking, and here also I found great delights, of which the chief, I think, was the discovery that the captain of one of the barges which brought him timber was a certain William Beasley, of Oxford, who had served my father as bailiff and fisherman, and in other employments, as many as a single pair of his hands could discharge. With him I had much talk, and always counted this talk very precious, it being chiefly of home matters, so that only the actual going thither could by any means be more to be desired.

CHAPTER III.

OF THE PLAGUE AND OTHER MATTERS.

I WAS well content both with my lodging at Master Rushworth's, though I thought, doubtless for want of grace, he was too puritanically inclined, and with the school. Our good parson had grounded me so well in the rudiments of Latin that I took at the first a place beyond my years; and I used such diligence and ability, if I may say so much of myself, that I lost not this advantage afterwards. Twice in the year there was held an examination of the scholars, or, as they call it, probation; and they that acquit themselves well therein are nominated to a higher place. This promotion I never failed to gain, save the first time only, when I had been but three months in the school, and this in a form which had none other so young as I. I do believe, indeed, that even then I had earned promotion; but the usher kept me back of set purpose, thinking this to be the best for me, for which kindness, though it angered me at the time,

I have since been most grateful. In the end it served me well, for, not to be tedious by dwelling over long on such matters, I had obtained at the first probation of 1636, of which year I shall shortly have more to say, a most excellent place in the school, being promoted into the fourth form, in which there was not, I remember, one scholar but had, at the least, six months more of age than myself.

But now there came a most grievous interruption, not to me only, which had been but a small matter, but to the prosperity of the whole nation. In the third year of my schooling (that is to say 1635) the plague broke out with no small violence in the City. And though it abated somewhat in the winter, as it commonly does, the cold seeming to discourage it, so that 'twas hoped it would depart altogether, yet in the year following, so soon as the spring-time began, it grew to such a height as had never before been known, so far as the memory of living man could reach. But there had been worse before, the Black Death, to wit, which left, 'twas said, scarce a tenth part of the people alive, and the Sweating sickness in the days of King Henry VIII. From this visitation the school suffered greatly. I do not say that many scholars actually perished of the sickness, for of these there were not, I take it, more than three or four at the most. But our numbers were sadly minished; for none came from the country, parents fearing to send their children into the midst of so deadly an infection, and of the London scholars also many were kept at home, lest, mixing with their fellows, they should either take the disease or convey it upon their clothes. It was a dismal sight to see the classes grow smaller, I may say, day after day. And when any boy was seen to be absent, there were rumours that he was dead of the plague; and though these, as I have said, were, for the most part, not true, yet we that remained were not the less troubled. At the last, when our numbers had dwindled down to a third or thereabouts of the full, came down an order from the Court that the school be shut. And this was done on the seventeenth of May, 1636.

I remember that we heard this news with a great shout of joy; for boys would rejoice in holiday though it should be brought about by the ending of the world; and now there was prospect of such a holiday as never had been known; and indeed the scholars were not again assembled together for the space of a year and five months, though Mr. Edwards, the chief master, taught some boys during that whole time, lest the school altogether ceasing to be, its property should be diverted elsewhere. But I was too young to be one of these.

As for myself, there was no small questioning what had better be done with me. My father indeed, as soon as there was talk of the school being shut up, had sent word that I should come home to him. But this was not easy to be done. For there was great fear throughout the country lest travellers from London should bring the infection of the disease with them, so that the roads were diligently watched, and all that were suspected of hailing thence were forthwith sent back, sometimes not without much maltreatment. This being so the river was the only highway that was left open. On this travellers were not hindered, provided only that they did not go forth from their boat into the villages round about. And by this highway I did in the end return home.

On the eleventh of June, for I remember that it was election day at the school, though the customary festivities were intermitted by reason of the plague, comes Richard Beasley with his barge, having with him a load of timber, and what I counted of more worth by far, the commandment from my father that I should return with him. And this I did about a sennight after, when he had finished the unloading of his cargo. We were six days on our journey, and I think that I never had so delightful a time. First it was no small joy to be quit for a time of London, which was indeed in those days a most dreadful place. None were seen in the streets save such as had urgent business; and these walked at such speed as if death were after them, (as indeed in a sense it was,) holding a handkerchief or pomander with some scent, recommended by the faculty, to their noses, as a safeguard against infection. As for the gallants in their brave attire and the fair matrons and damsels that had been wont to throng the public ways, they were invisible,

OF THE PLAGUE AND OTHER MATTERS.   31

and the church bells never gave forth a merry peal, but were tolling continually, till indeed this was forbidden as augmenting the terror of the citizens. And there passed continually along the streets the funerals of the wealthier sort of people and their families. But as for the poorer, the dead-cart carried them to their burying places, and this I, lying awake at night, have often heard rumbling awfully along, and also the cry of the men asking, whenever they saw a house shut up, whether there was anything for them. And I must confess, though it be to my discredit, that Master Rushworth and his wife wearied me with over long exercises of prayer such as they thought fitted for the occasion, not remembering my tender years. It may easily be concluded therefore that I was sufficiently glad to depart from London. And for the journey itself, it was, as I have said, delightful beyond all compare. We set out on the nineteenth of June, being, as I remember, a Saturday, for Robert, though he had all things ready, would not begin his journey on a Friday, a scrupulousness at which I was not a little offended, being above all things desirous to depart. That night we lay at Richmond, and the day following also, being a Sunday, on which day William Beasley was steadfast not to travel. He would say that, if a man cared not for his own soul, knowing it not to be worth a groat, he should have regard to his beast, which must be priced at twenty shillings at the least.

We travelled without any mischance save that at Bray, where the river is more than ordinary shallow, William Beasley's son having had the rudder in charge, ran the barge on a shoal, and would have had a great whipping from his father but that I took the blame on myself; which was indeed but fair, for I was distracting the lad with my talk when he needed all his wits for his work. At some of the ferries we had to serve ourselves, for the ferrymen would not venture themselves near to those that might be bringing, as they thought, the infection of the disease from London. And when we would buy anything from the town and villages, as eggs and milk, or the like, we left the money at an appointed place (the custom having grown up in former visitations), dropping it into a bowl of water; and the country folk afterwards brought their goods. And then, with a "God save you!" given and returned, we went on our way. 'Twas a doleful thing to be so shunned, as if we had been lepers; yet I could not blame the people, knowing that the plague had been carried down from London to the utter destruction of many villages. For a village, if it once take the infection, will often, for lack of ministration to the sick, suffer worse than the town. But once only did the riverside people show us any hostility; and this was at Wallingford, where they stoned us from the bridge, but without doing any considerable hurt.

But notwithstanding these incommodities, 'twas a most delightsome time such as I have ever remembered with pleasure, and shall remember so long as life be left to me. I have seen evil days since then—Thames running red with civil blood, if I may so speak, and all this fair land of England disturbed with the strife of brothers fighting against brothers. But these days had not then come; and if there were signs and tokens of the storms that were gathering, and such doubtless there were for them that had discerning eyes. I was too young to take note of them. And I was newly come from a city where there was but little talk of aught but pestilence and death, and doleful sights and sounds about me on every side, so that the country scenes, full of gladness and life, into which I had, as it were, escaped, were the more exceedingly delightful. Nor is there, methinks, a fairer thing in England, when one is once past the environs of the city, than Thames, nor any season in which Thames is more to be admired than that early summer in which we were then journeying. For the trees are in their fullest leaf and not yet withered at all by the heat, and the river banks are bright with flowers, as the forget-me-nots and the flags, both yellow and purple, and the water-plants, of more kinds than I can name, gay with blossom; also one may see the water-hens and the grebes, leading about their newly hatched broods, and the swans, carrying on their backs their cygnets, whose brown plumes show forth tenderly from out the silvery white, and the halcyons with their comely colours of green and red, carrying food to their young. All these and many more things that I have not the wit duly to describe did I see and note, young though I was, during our voyage.

Also as we went along William Beasley would cast a bait—a moth, may be, or a slug, or sometimes, to my no small wonder, a morsel of cheese—under the boughs that hung over the water, and draw out thence mighty big chevenders, or, as some call them, chubs. This he did with a most dexterous hand; ay, and having caught them, he would cook them no less skilfully, so that this fish, which I have since found to be tasteless, made as dainty meat as could be desired; or was it that the flavour was not in the dish but in its surroundings? And when we had accomplished our journey for the day, he would prepare an angle for me, and teach me to catch roaches and perches. And once, I remember, when I was pulling to me a roach that was on the hook, a pike of some six or seven pounds laid hold upon him, and would not let go, so bold and ravenous was he. And William Beasley, in the deftest manner that ever I beheld (and I have seen the same thing oft attempted since, but never accomplished), put a hand-net under the beast, and brought him in.

And he would have it, being one of the kindest hearts that ever lived, that I had caught the pike. And we had a great feast off him; 'twas excellent meat, white and firm, though somewhat weedy, said William; but I noted nothing amiss. Near to Oxford my father met me, and carried me home, where I lived with much content until the time when, as I have said, the Merchant Taylors' School was opened again, a space of fifteen months and more. 'Twas not lost time so far as learning was concerned, for our good parson took me in hand again and taught me. And, indeed, he had been teaching my sister Dorothy, so that she was a match, ay, and more than a match, for me, being both older and of a nimbler wit. But being the tenderest soul alive, and fearing that I should be grieved if she outstripped me too far, she would hold back; and I, thinking that I could vanquish her, and being sometimes by her suffered so to do, did my utmost. Verily I believe that I had not learned more at the school itself, though my preceptors there were diligent both with the voice and the rod, in which latter instrument of learning they had such faith as Solomon himself,

OF THE PLAGUE AND OTHER MATTERS. 37

who, methinks, has much affliction of youth to answer for, could not have excelled. Nor did I gain in learning only, but also in strength of body and health, in which, haply, I had fared ill had I been cooped within the City walls.

In the year 1643—for that I be not tedious to them that shall read this history I shall say no more of my schooldays—I, being then eighteen years of age and not unfit, if I may say so much of myself, to compare with the best scholars of the said school, did hope for my election to a vacancy in the College of St. John the Baptist at Oxford. But of this hope I was disappointed, not altogether, methinks, of my own fault. It came about in this manner. About the beginning of May comes a letter from the President and Fellows of the College, wherein they write that they dare not, by reason of the troubles of the times, venture so far as to come to London that they might take part, as their custom was, in the election of scholars to their College. So it turned out, to cut the matter short, that the Company held the said election privately by themselves. Now my uncle, Master Harland aforesaid, died about this time; and as during his life he had been somewhat masterful, ruling most things according to his pleasure, so now, being dead, there was, so to speak, a turn of the tide against him and his, by which turn I suffered. They also to whom I looked for help, to wit the President and Fellows of St. John's College, were absent for the cause that I have already set forth. And so it happened that when it came to the election I had but two voices. And this I say not by way of complaint against them that ordered the election, nor of murmuring against God, but because I desire to set forth what befell me, and, as far as I can, the causes of the same. As for murmuring, indeed, I doubt much whether I lost any great profit in this matter, though I will confess that it was at the time no small disappointment and bitterness. For the same cause that hindered the Fellows of the College from coming to London, hindered also the scholars that were then elected from going to Oxford; so that it was a long time before they were admitted to their preferment. And, in truth, when they were admitted, it was but an unprofitable matter, for the College was almost at the point of dissolution for lack of means, many of its tenants not being able to pay their rents, and some that had the ability making pretence of the troubles of the times to cover their dishonesty. And thus my schooldays came to an end.

CHAPTER IV.

OF THINGS AT HOME.

I HAVE said but little hitherto of our civil troubles; and, indeed, they touched us but lightly within the walls of our school. I had almost said that they did but give a new name to our sports; for whereas our factions—such as a school commonly has—had before called themselves by the names of Greeks and Trojans, or Romans and Carthaginians, according as Homer or Livy were most in our hands, so now we were King's men and Parliament's men, or Rebels, as we that were of the loyal faction would often style these latter. But it must be confessed that there was something beyond the ordinary of veritable anger in these combats; so that once or twice the partisans appeared in their places in school with broken heads or other damage, and would doubtless have so done more often but for fear of our master, Mr. Edwards, who did mete out a most severe and impartial justice to all that presumed to disturb the peace of his realm. The City folk were for the most part friends to the Parliament, and their faction had the majority of the scholars. Yet the King, too, had those that stood stoutly by him; of whom I, being tall and strong and expert in all bodily exercises, was chosen to be the leader. I do remember what a fierce battle we had on the fifth day of January, in the year 1642, which was the day following that on which the King would have seized the five members. So hot were we about it that we noted not our master coming upon us and finding us *in flagrante delicto*. A battle of the bees, says Virgil, is stayed by the throwing of a little dust, and we were pacified by the first sound of his voice; and, indeed, though I have had experience of sundry sights and sounds of terror, I know nothing so terrible as the voice of a schoolmaster, so he be one that hath what all have not, the true secret of rule. He had noted down the names of all the chief combatants before we were aware of him; nor did one of them escape due punishment.

As for myself, being, as I suppose, of such an age, and may be strength that I could scarce be flogged, he set me to English the first book of the *Pharsalia* of Lucan, which treats, as all know, of the civil wars of Rome. 'Tis choice verse, doubtless, but passing difficult—or so at least I found it—and gave me but scant leisure between Epiphany-tide ('twas on the fifth day of January that the tumult was) and the beginning of Lent, a space of near upon two months. So much, then, for our mimicries of war. But now, coming home—which I did not long after my hopes at the school had been, as I have said, disappointed—I found the reality. And, indeed, on my journey, which was not accomplished without peril, I had seen something of it. For coming by way of Thame—which I was advised was to be preferred because some troopers of the Prince Rupert lay at Fawley near to Henley-upon-Thames and harried all travellers with small respect of parties—and staying to bait my horse at the inn, I heard that a notable man was lying dead in one of the chambers. ('Twas Midsummer Day, I remember.) This was Master John Hampden, who had been shot in the shoulder upon Chalgrove Field six days before, and being carried to Thame died there on the very day on which I chanced to pass through. His name had been much in men's mouths, and was not a little regarded even by them who judged him to have erred (of which number was I); and it troubled me not a little to hear that he had been slain, though he was an enemy to the King. I had heard before of such things, and, indeed, at Edgehill, where the King's men and the army of the Parliament under my Lord Essex had fought with doubtful success, thousands had been slain and wounded; but now I saw death close at hand for the first time; and it moved me mightily.

I found my father greatly discomposed, though at first he sought to hide his trouble by jest and banter. The first evening after my coming, as we sat by the fire, for he was one that even at midsummer would have a fire be it ever so small, he smoking his pipe, which was a custom he had learned of the Germans, he began thus with me:

"I am for the King, as you well know, son Philip; but 'twould be well if you could be persuaded in your conscience that the Parliament has the right."

I could say nothing, being struck dumb, so to speak, with astonishment. Then he went on:

"'Tis the fashion hereabouts to order things in this way, and has been since these present troubles began, as doubtless you would have known but for being away in London. See now there is Master Holmes at Upcott, t'other side of the river; he is for the Parliament, and Geoffrey his son is for the King; and Sir William Tresham, of Parton, is a staunch Cavalier, but William Tresham the younger e'en as staunch a Roundhead."

"Nay, father," said I, finding my tongue at last, "I cannot conceive that I should be found different from you in this matter."

Then he laughed and said: "Your schooling has not made your wits as nimble as might have been looked for. Dost not see how the matter stands? If the King prevail, no harm shall befall Upcott, for is not Geoffrey loyal? nor any if the Parliament get the better, seeing that Master Holmes himself hath ever been zealous for it. And for Sir William, 'tis but the same story told the other way. Master Tresham goes in the new ways, but the good knight his father loves the old; and it cannot but be that the one or the other is in the right. What say you? I am too old to change, and the world would wonder if, when I have fought for his Majesty's house, I should now turn against him; but you have been brought up among the citizens, with whom he is, I am told, in but small favour. Shall we make a Master Doubleface between us, and make the inheritance sure whatever may befall?"

What I should have said I know not, for though the matter of his speech was utterly strange to me, he showed no token but of being utterly serious; but I must have showed some distemper in my face, for before I could answer, he broke in upon me:

"Nay, son Philip, answer not. 'Tis enough. I did ill to jest on such a matter, which is indeed too serious for any words but those of soberness. Come, let us take counsel together. To live here is a thing past all enduring, at least for any man that cares not to run with the hare and hunt with the hounds. An I could welcome the Parliament's men one day and the King's men the next, I might make a good profit out of both, and so fare well. But such is not to my taste. My purpose then is to put my sword to the grindstone again, and to take service with the King. I am not what I was, but I am not too old to strike a blow for the good cause. The farm I shall leave to John Vickers. 'Tis an honest man enough, but he cares not, I do believe in my heart, one groat for King or Parliament, so that he gets in the hay and corn without damage of blight or hindrance of weather. I have made a covenant with him, not in writing, but by word of mouth—for be he not honest, as indeed I do trust he is, writing will not bind him more than speech—that he shall pay so much by the year, according as the price of corn shall be. 'Twill be, as I reckon, about eighty pounds; of this I shall keep twenty for my own use, so that I shall not need to trouble the King's chest, which has, I take it, enough, and more than enough, to do. Your mother's portion is in the hands of Nicholas Barratt, a maltster of Reading, who pays six pounds per centum, making thirty pounds by the year in all. And this, with the residue of that which comes from John Vickers she must make suffice for herself and your sister Dorothy and you. And now for yourself."

At that I brake in: "That matter is soon sped. My place is nowhere but with my father."

"Nay," said he, "you have forgotten half the commandment, which runs: 'Honour thy father *and thy mother.*' Thy mother and sister must needs dwell in Oxford, and I should not be content to leave them there without some man of their kindred to take their part. I doubt neither the loyalty nor the courage of those that serve his Majesty, but there are not a few among them that are somewhat loose of life, which is, indeed, but too common a fault of soldiers. You will soon see for yourself that a fair maid, such as is your sister Dorothy, could scarce stir abroad had she not you to bear her company, nor would I have you at your age in a camp; 'tis not a place for a lad, as you still are, for all your inches and broad shoulders. 'Tis the time for learning and fitting yourself for your work in life; for these wars will come to an end some day, though I doubt not that they will last so long that this realm shall be almost brought to ruin. And what would you do, being left at two or three and twenty years of age, having learnt nothing and forgotten much, and 'all thy occupation gone,' as Will Shakespeare hath it?"

It matters not what I said in answer to this. I did not yield at once, but debated the matter for awhile, being thus disappointed of my hope. But 'twas all to no purpose, for my father was resolute, and I could not but acknowledge in my heart that he had the right.

The next day, therefore, my mother and sister having for some time past bestirred themselves to get all things ready for removal, we left our home and journeyed to Oxford, lodging for a time at the *Maidenhead*, which is a tavern opposite to Lincoln College, till we could find a convenient dwelling in the town. This was no easy matter, for Oxford was full, it may be said to overflowing, with courtiers and soldiers. But at last, by the kindness of Mistress Wood, widow of Thomas Wood, that had died the year before, having been always a good friend to my father, we found a little house not far from Merton College. 'Twas but a poor place, having only two chambers with one parlour and a kitchen, with no garden but a little yard only (a thing which troubled the women folk much, not only because it stinted them of air and exercise, the streets being scarce fit for them to walk in, but because they were constrained to buy such trifles as parsley and mint, and everything, though but the veriest trifle, that was needed for the household). Yet we were right glad to find even this shelter, having almost begun to despair; and, indeed, we scarce suffered the former occupiers, the widow and daughter of a King's officer, newly slain in the wars, to depart before we filled their places, so fearful were we lest someone else should be beforehand with us. Nor indeed, for very shame, could we complain, seeing that Mistress Wood lived in a house that was scarce better than ours, her own having been given up to my Lord Colepepper, Master of the Rolls. Nor was it a slight matter that this narrow dwelling suited our shallow purse, for shallow it was when money was so scarce and all articles of provision so dear as we found them to be in Oxford. And here let me say that neither did Master Barratt fail to pay interest on my mother's fortune, nor John Vickers his yearly rent, most scrupulously calculated according to the current price of corn. The worthy man also did send my mother many gifts of fruit and butter, and fowls and game in its season, so that although we had no superfluity, we never lacked, but could give to many that needed. Of these, indeed, there was no small number in Oxford, some of them being persons of good estate, that, having less honest tenants than John Vickers, could get no return of rent from their lands.

Me my father entered at Lincoln College, with the Rector of which, Dr. Paul Hood, he had a friendship (or I should rather say an acquaintance) of old standing. By good fortune it happened that the place of one of the four Trappes scholars fell empty beyond expectation, the scholar having taken service with the King and being killed in battle. The news came on the very day of my entering, and as I had gained some credit by answering, and much praise from them that examined me, and no one else desired the place, the vacancy being, as I have said, without expectation, I was chosen to it by a unanimous voice. 'Twas no great matter, fifty-two shillings by the year only; but 'twas, nevertheless, a welcome promotion.

CHAPTER V.

OF THINGS AT OXFORD.

'Twas a stirring time at Oxford when I first began my residence in the University. The King had there his headquarters, and there was scarce a day but messengers came bearing news, good or bad, of the war that was being carried forward in every part of England. Also a Parliament sat—I speak now of the first year of my residence, that is to say from October, 1643, to the same month of the year following—at which were present some hundred and fifty, reckoning both Commoners and Peers. But of these matters I shall say more hereafter; at the present I will speak rather of things concerning my own College.

Lincoln College is a fair building, of an honourable antiquity, there being six Colleges only that are older than it and ten that are of newer date, but it has only a poor estate, its first founder having died before he could fulfil his purpose, and other benefactors, for such have not been wanting to us, not wholly making good his unwilling defect. Its chief ornament is the chapel, which is in the Gothic style (a style, in my judgment, much to be preferred to the Italian novelty which many in these days prefer), fairly lined with cedar, and illustrated with windows most handsomely painted. These windows were brought from Italy at the instance of the builder, Dr. Williams, sometime Bishop of Lincoln and Lord Keeper, whose liberality in this matter is the more to be commended because he is not even of this University, but visitor only of the College in right of his bishopric. My chamber was under the roof at the top of the chapel staircase, and had a fair prospect of the church of All Saints, which, in a sort, belongs to the College, and of that part of the town which lies toward the river.

On the first day of November, being All Saints' Day, we—that is to say, all the members of the College then residing, from the

Rector to the Clerks—walked in solemn procession to this church, where prayers were said, and a sermon preached by Master Richard Chalfont, the Sub-Rector, the Rector, to whom the duty of this discourse more properly belongs, pleading inability by reason of illness; but 'tis thought that 'twas an excuse rather than a reason, and that, being a prudent man, as was most abundantly proved by his keeping his preferment through all the changes of the times, he chose rather to be silent in so critical a juncture of affairs. We looked for a discourse on political matters from Master Chalfont, who was very hot for the King; but he preached on no such subject, but on the pleasures which shall be enjoyed in heaven. Some thought the theme ill-chosen, but others, to whose opinion I incline, greatly commended this choice, saying that of politics we hear enough, and more than enough, in the market-place, and that higher things are more befitting the sanctuary. 'Twas a most academical discourse. I remember he told us that we should there, among other good things, find repaired all damages that time or accident has made in the remains of antiquity, reading, for example, the comedies of Eupolis, a contemporary, but elder, of Aristophanes, which have been most lamentably lost, and such books of Livy and Tacitus as are wanting to the manuscripts, and solving also problems of geometry and algebra which are beyond our present skill. I thought that many of the auditors listened to these prognostications with blank faces, as thinking, doubtless, that they had here upon earth more than a sufficiency of such things.

The day was kept as a high day in the College, provision beyond the ordinary being made both for dinner and supper in the hall. There was no lack of jollity, though I heard some complain, in a doubtful manner, of the change which had been wrought since the last Gaudy (for such is the name, being short for *gaudeamus*, which they give to this festivity) was held. Then there had been a goodly show of plate, none drinking save out of silver; but this was now all gone, being melted down for the pay of his Majesty's soldiers, and our cups were of earthenware.

On Shrove Tuesday, which, in the year 1644

(to which I am now come), fell on the second day of March, there was held what, if I may borrow a word from a venerable custom of antiquity, may be styled the initiation of the Freshmen. The fire in the hall was made earlier than ordinary; the Fellows also went to supper before six, and made an end sooner than at other times, so leaving the hall to the liberty of the undergraduates, but not without an admonitory hint given by the Sub-Rector, as having charge of the discipline of the College that all things should be carried on in good order. While they were at supper in the hall, the cook was making hot caudle at the charge of the Freshmen, who, I should have said, are all that have come into the University since the Shrove Tuesday last before. (Caudle, I should say, for the sake of those that are not learned in such matters, is a drink made of oatmeal flour, mixed in water, with sherry wine.) This being ready, and all the undergraduates and servants being assembled in the hall, each Freshman, in his turn, according to his seniority, was constrained to make a speech, but not without preparation, for notice was given that it would be required of him on Candlemas Day. First, he plucked off his gown and bands, and made himself look as like a low fellow as he could; some, I must needs confess, acquitting themselves in this respect with much success. This done, he made his speech, being placed on a form, which was set on the high table, touching with such wit as he was master of on the persons and characters of his brother Freshmen and on the servants of the College, the latter more especially, being a game at which the very feeblest hawks could fly. If he did well, speaking in an audible voice, and with a good fluency of words and passable matter, there was given him a cup of caudle, and no salted drink; if he did indifferently, neither ill nor well, some caudle and some salted drink; but if he was dull, or halted in his speech, then he had nothing but salted drink; that is to say, beer, with salt therein, and tucks* to boot. This done, the senior cook administered to him an oath, which began thus: "Item tu jurabis, quod *penniless bench* non visitabis," but the rest I forget. As for "penniless bench," 'tis a seat by St. Martin's

---

* A "tuck" was a pinch, given with finger and thumb under the lip, and sometimes drawing blood.

Church (which is called also Carfax), where the hucksters and butter-women sit. This oath each Freshman took over an old shoe, which when he had kissed with due solemnity, he put on again his gown and bands, and was duly admitted into the worshipful company of seniors. This was doubtless but foolish work, though I doubt me much whether now, when we are so far wiser that all such festivities are forbidden, we be much better. I trust, at the least, that none will think the worse of me if I boast that I did my fooling so graciously that the cup that was given to me was of caudle only, and no admixture of salt.

Such sportiveness is to be looked for in the young; and, indeed, did their gay temper and light heart lead them no further than into such diversions, there were small cause for blame; it may be alleged also, there was something academical, though turned to purposes of mirth, in these our enforced disputings. So much may not be said of all the sports to which the younger sort were addicted. Some were given to the fighting of cocks, a barbarous thing in my judgment, though long custom has appropriated it to the last day before Lent, so that some would think the world itself shaken in its foundations were this absent; but, be it good or bad, 'twill be acknowledged that 'tis not a seemly thing for the quadrangle of a College, where I have seen it practised, and that not once or twice only. The baiting of badgers also with terrier dogs was much followed. As for hunting the fox, it was interrupted by the war; for who could follow the chase when he was like to find the King's men in one village and the Parliament's soldiers in the next? So the war brought peace, I may say, to the foxes; but the hares and partridges had little rest, for the disturbed times gave excuse to many for carrying fire-arms, which they could use, as occasion served, for their own purposes. But who could know whether a musket were loaded with a bullet that might kill a man, or with small shot that might bring down a beast or a bird? And if 'twas a bullet that it bore, what was to hinder it being used against a fat hart or a roebuck? The keepers of game had, I take it, an ill time in these days; indeed, their occupation was in many places wholly given up. And if such abuses have commonly been found among the scholars of the University, now they prevailed tenfold more. But of this more in its proper place.

But what shall be said of the seniors, the Masters of Arts. Before I came to Oxford I had thought, in my simplicity, that these were all grave and reverend persons, given to books and study, that, as our new poet, Master John Milton, has it, did "outwatch the Bear;" but I soon learnt to think otherwise; and here I will take leave to tell a true tale, from which may be seen how some of these reverend seniors did demean themselves. But that there were grave and pious men even in the worst times I shall not deny.

There was in the College a certain Master of Arts, by name Thomas Smith, a violent person, who had been admonished and punished for diverse offences and disorders, of which it was counted not the least heinous that he kept dogs in his chamber, and would neither remove them nor himself when warned by the Rector so to do. Master Smith had a quarrel, in which private enmity was doubtless aggravated by public differences, with another Master of Arts, also dwelling in the College, by name Nicholas North, and a minister. They had had diverse fallings out in time past, but the gravest of all, by reason of which Master Smith came near to being expelled from the College (and doubtless had been so but for the favour of some Fellows that were of his way of thinking in matters of Church and State), was this. It will be best told in their own words, as I afterwards found it written down; and first for Master North's account:

"On Monday night, immediately after I had supped in the buttery, going in the new quadrangle, I heard a door shut, and thinking it had been mine, said to him that came forth, 'Who is there?' Master Smith answered, 'Who are you that examine me?' I replied, 'I do not examine you.' He said, 'You are a base rogue for examining me.' When I heard him say so, fearing he would fall upon me, I hasted with all the speed I could to my chamber; but, as I opened the door, Master Smith caught hold of my gown and said, 'Sirrah! Come out; you are a base rogue for examining me!' Said I, 'You cannot prove me such. I pray you let me go; I have nought to say to you.' 'Ay,' said he, 'but I have something to say to you;' and taking me by the ear and hair of the head with one hand, he plucked out a cudgel that was under his gown, and making into the chamber upon me, struck me with the cudgel upon the head. About the third blow it broke in two. After that he struck me half-a-dozen blows with that piece he had in his hand, and when I wrested this out of his hand he laid me about the face with his fist. There being two in my chamber, I asked them whether they were not ashamed to see me beaten in my own chamber, and would not call company to take him off. After a while came Master Chalfont* running in and took him off from me, and three several times did Master Smith call me 'base rogue' and run in upon me, and was taken off three times by Master Chalfont; and when I entreated him to go out of my chamber he called me a base, inferior rogue, and would not go out till he had every piece of his stick."

Now for Master Smith's story:

* This Richard Chalfont was expelled in the year 1648. He was minister to the company of English Merchants in Rotterdam.

"Coming out of my chamber on Monday night, about seven of the clock, I met Master North coming forth from his chamber. He said, 'What are you, sir?' I answered, 'What is that to you?' He drew me to his chamber door. I asked him why he used me so. He said that I had taken something out of his chamber. I told him that he was an unworthy man, and I would make him know himself; and Master North being within his chamber, dared me to fall on him, saying 'Strike me if thou durst!' Then I perceived a bed-staff in his gown sleeve, he holding the little end in his hand and the great end downwards. Thereupon, having a stick in my hand, I struck at him, and hitting him on the top of the head, broke the stick in pieces."

Here Master Smith was questioned how he came to have a stick, which it is against rule and custom to carry. He said, "I was newly come out of town from the company of some friends, and by the way was jostled from the walk by two scholars, and having shortly to return, not knowing whether I might be abused again, took the stick under my gown."

Further, in answer to Master North, he said, "I do not absolutely know whether I did after strike him in his chamber, but might have so done, partly by heat of passion and ill-language that was given me, and partly defending myself."

There was no small discussion about this matter, but in the end Master Smith was commanded to pay ten pounds to Master North for the wrong done to him (of which sum Master North was persuaded to abate a third part), and to make a public submission and acknowledgment in the chapel in the face of all the society assembled. And these two things he did.

Such were the manners of the time, and afterwards, as will be seen, they grew worse rather than better.

CHAPTER VI.

OF THE KING'S GOING TO WORCESTER.

MY father was well remembered by some of the older sort about the King's person, as also by the Prince Rupert, elder son of the Princess Elizabeth, and so nephew to the King, who, when he was a child, had greatly favoured him. Hence, without any delay, he obtained the commission of a captain of horse. Indeed, being a man of capacity and of some experience in military matters, while most of the King's officers were wholly raw and uninstructed in the art of war, he had more weight in council than of right belonged to his rank; nor do I doubt but that, had it not pleased God to order things otherwise, he would have been promoted to a principal command. Indeed he had, very soon after his first joining the army, the chief direction of his regiment, the colonel being a young gentleman of quality, that had none of the virtues belonging to a soldier save courage only, unless it is to be counted as a virtue that he knew his own ignorance, and gave a ready ear to the counsel of wiser men.

For myself, I gave my attention to things academical, and was a diligent student, exercising an industry which, I make bold to say, few others in the University excelled. This, it must be confessed, was not altogether of my own free choice ; but my father would have it so. "Stick to your books," he would say, "son Philip, so long as you can." Thus for the present time you will serve your cause most effectually. If the need come for your hand, I shall not spare to call you ; but remember that it is easier to take up the sword than to lay it down." Nevertheless, with my father's consent ; that I might be ready for such occasion when soever it might come, I learnt my exercises, both as a foot-soldier and a trooper. (I had learnt to ride while yet a child, perfecting myself in the art during my long compelled absence from school in the time of the plague.) I had, through the bounty of my father, arms of my own, namely, a steel cap, a back and breast-piece and a pike, with the other appurtenances. We trained commonly in the quadrangle of New College, the warden whereof, Dr. Robert Pink, deputy vice-chancellor, was a zealous King's man. There was a school kept in the cloisters of New College, wherein were taught first the singing boys of the chapel (with which scarce any other in England can be compared), and also other youth of the town. And I remember what ado the ushers had with the lads on the training days. There was no holding them in their school on these occasions; neither tasks nor the terror of the lash could hinder them from seeing and following the soldiers.

As this year (1644) went on, it was more and more manifest that the King was in a great strait. My father would have it that he was ill served by his advisers, especially in their continual changing of their plans, which, when they had settled them after long and painful debate, they would often unsettle without sufficient cause. I have, indeed, heard him say, "If his Majesty would but trust his own judgment, which is indeed better than can be found in many of them that pretend to be his advisers, and having once come by a resolution would carry it out determinately, 'twould be well for him and for his kingdom." Whatever the cause, it came to pass that in the month of May the King's affairs were in such ill case that he was like to be besieged in Oxford. The forces that he had with him were scarce a third part as numerous as those that the Parliament had arrayed against him; nor could he look for any present help from elsewhere, Prince Rupert being on his march to relieve my Lord Derby (besieged in his castle of Lathom), and Prince Maurice having sat down before Lyme in the county of Dorset, a little fisher-town which he was not like to take, and which, if taken, had been but of small account. The King therefore had to retire his troops from Reading. Abingdon also, which is not more than five miles from Oxford, was abandoned, though this was against the King's desire and even command expressly given; so that all Berkshire now was in the hands of Parliament by their two commanders, the Earl of Essex and Sir William Waller, and the King

OF THE KING'S GOING TO WORCESTER.

was forced to draw his whole force of horse and foot on the north side of Oxford; nay more, the Parliament came into Oxfordshire, my Lord Essex getting over the Thames at Sandford Ferry (which is three miles away from Oxford), and halting on Bullingdon Green, whence he sent parties of horse up to the very gates of the city. This was on the twenty-ninth day of May. Meanwhile Sir William Waller also had crossed the Thames and was come as far as Eynsham, where he lay at my father's house, but did no damage, but was, on the contrary, cause of no small profit to John Vickers, and so through him to my father; the said John selling to him and his company poultry and eggs and the like at such a price as did, in a way, avenge the King's wrongs. Now, therefore, the King was well nigh surrounded, for some of my Lord Essex's horse had gone forward as far as Woodstock, so that there was but one vacant space left in the circle which the enemy had not yet occupied, to wit, between Eynsham and Woodstock, and this space was of not more than six miles.

So desperate indeed was the situation of

affairs that there were many now who counselled the King that he should give himself up to the Earl of Essex, to which advice he gave this answer, as my father told me who heard the very words as they came from his mouth. "'Tis possible I shall be found in the hands of the Earl of Essex, but I shall be dead first."

On the third day of June, at eleven of the clock in the forenoon, as I sat in my chamber, comes my father to me. I was reading, I remember, in the twenty-seventh book of the Histories of Livy of how the Consul Livius made a sudden march to join forces with his colleague against Hasdrubal, then threatening to combine his army with Hannibal's to the great danger of the commonwealth of Rome. My father had a more cheerful look than I had seen in him since my coming home. Indeed, he was one of them to whom the bare prospect of danger is a singular great delight, so that the whistling of a bullet near to him would rouse him as a draught of wine does other men, and would change his ordinary mood, which was somewhat grave and reserved, to a most uncommon gaiety and mirth. Says he,

Friar Bacon's House.

"Son Philip, I see you are set to pull down Friar Bacon's house about your ears.* Nevertheless, put away your books, if you have a mind for a ride to-night. My colonel is sick of a fever, which he contracted, I take it, from toasting the King too zealously last night at St. John's College, where they drink perilously deep. 'Tis not a serious ailment, but it hinders him at the present time from the saddle ; and by the King's special word I am to have command of the regiment. Further, the King said, 'Thou wilt need some one to carry messages and the like, a young man of courage and discretion, and a bold rider. Dost know of such a one?' Then I said—let it not turn your head to hear such good opinions of yourself— 'Sire, I have a son who would do his utmost to please your Majesty.' Then he would know who you were; but when he heard that you were a scholar, his face clouded somewhat, and he said, 'A scholar is best at his books. 'Tis not the least evil of this most unhappy war that it has changed this seat of learning into a

* The tradition was that the house would fall when a more learned man than the Friar should pass beneath it.

barrack of soldiers. Where shall I find preachers and counsellors if I turn my scholars into troopers?' But when I told his Majesty that you were diligent at your books, he said, 'Well, if the lad will take this ride as a holiday and return hereafter to his books, it shall be as you wish. Will you answer for him?' And when I said that I would it was settled that you should come. But mind, son Philip, that you do not falsify my word. And now I will have a word with Master Hood, your Rector, for the King has promised that you shall have dispensation for the rest of your term if perchance you have not kept it." And, indeed, I had kept but half of Trinity term, which begins on the Wednesday after Whit Sunday. The Rector made no hindrance, being always amenable to them that are in authority. Only he would not give me permission to be absent under his hand, which my father would gladly have had. "'Tis no need," he said; but I do suspect that he would not do aught that might be used in evidence against him. He is a good man, of wise carriage and conduct, and learning sufficient for his place; but 'tis cardinal doctrine with him that

he must be Rector of Lincoln College. 'Tis not altogether ill with the world, he thinks, so long as that be so. Hitherto he has kept his profits and dignities while many have lost them, as I shall show hereafter; and if, to speak profanely, Fortune shall give another turn to her wheel, and the King have his own again, I doubt not we shall find Master Hood* at the top in as good case as ever.

My father had, with no small difficulty, bespoken a horse for me, and when I had settled my small affairs at College, I went down to William Barnes his stables in S. Aldate's so as to make acquaintance with him. The first sight of him dashed me somewhat. He was, I thought, over small for me, having not more than thirteen hands in height, while my stature exceeded six feet by three inches and more. But his colour troubled me more than his littleness, for he was of the spotted kind, such as they commonly use in shows. William Barnes perceived that I was ill at ease, and would comfort me. "Nay,

* Paul Hood held the Rectorship of Lincoln College from 1620 to 1668, and therefore outlasted the change from King to Parliament, and from Parliament again to King. No other head of a house was equally compliant or equally long lived.

Master," he said, "'tis an excellent beast for all his queer look. A good horse is ever of a good colour, say I; and as for strength it does not always go with bigness. I warrant he would carry three of you, if his back were long enough. And if your legs be over long, you must shorten your stirrups." Nor, indeed, were his commendations ill bestowed. It must be confessed that there was much laughter when I was first seen on his back, and laughter is sometimes almost as ill to bear as blows. But he never failed me in any need. He never flinched at the noise of the cannons—no, not when he heard it for the first time, whereas there were, I noted, many horses that could never be trusted, but that they would carry their riders clean off the field, to their no small discredit, or straight into the enemy, to their no small danger. But Spot—for so I called the good beast—was ever steady and obedient to the rein, and if provender were short he was content to wait, nor yet failed in strength, however long the day's work might be. Poor Spot, he is with many another on Naseby Field. I am not ashamed to confess that though I had, God knows, other and heavier griefs that day, I shed tears to think I should see him no more. But I must return to the time of which I am now speaking.

Though my father had been secret as to the purpose of the ride, as he named it, to which he called me, I had little doubt what this might be. Yet was I somewhat mistaken. For thinking that the King was intending to go forth from Oxford, where, as I have said, he was near to being surrounded, to some part where he might have freer action, and to do this with a small company of followers, I found, coming down to the north gate, which I did about half-past eight on the evening, that there was a whole army assembled. There were, as I did afterwards discover, about 6,000 men, of whom the greater part were horse. The horse were drawn up in a very fair array in Port Meadow, which had been conveniently chosen for this purpose, as lying low and so being out of sight of the enemy. The foot soldiers, marching down the lane that runs by Aristotle's Well, there joined them; and so, about nine of the clock, when it was now beginning to grow dark, we set off, the horse, whereof my father's regiment was the foremost, being in front, and the footmen following after with as much haste as they might. And, indeed, besides that all were picked men, 'twas not a march in which any would desire to linger, so great was the danger lest the enemy's forces, being much more numerous, should close upon us. These, as I have before said, were on either side of us, but on the present occasion the army of Lord Essex was the more to be dreaded, seeing that it had pushed forward its outposts so far as Woodstock town, whereas we, marching by Picksey and Oxsey Mead, and over Worton Heath, skirted the very walls of Woodstock Park. Our chief care was concerning a certain bridge over the Evenlode River that is hard by the village of Long Hanborough, whether it were held by the enemy or no. For if it was so held we should have to fight for it, and if we fought it would be small odds whether we got the better or the worse, for we could scarce hope, being checked upon our way, to outstrip our pursuers. About midnight there was a consultation held among the leaders, whereof the

A Halt of Officers.

OF THE KING'S GOING TO WORCESTER. 77

outcome was this, that my father with two hundred horsemen, each carrying a musqueteer behind him, rode forward with as much speed as they could command, being specially chosen for their courage and for the strength and quickness of their horses. It was purposed that these should occupy and hold the bridge at Hanborough. With these I rode, and when we were come to the bridge, and by God's providence found it vacant, says my father to me, "Son Philip, ride back to the army with all the speed you can, and tell the good news to the King." So I rode, putting spurs to my horse, though indeed the good beast needed not spur nor whip; and when I arrived at the army I found the King, with whom was the whole inception and conduct of the affair from the beginning to the end, had ridden to the front. And when he saw me, careful and troubled as he was about the matter, he had much ado to keep from laughter, so strange a figure did we show. But when he heard my news, he said, "This is excellent good tidings; never came more welcome Mercury than thou. And that need be a marvellous good beast of thine, be his looks what they may, for thee to have gone and returned so speedily. But spare him now, and follow quietly."

There is no need to write of this march at length, though indeed it was marvellously well conceived and executed. Let it suffice then to say so much as follows. We proceeded without halt till the afternoon, when we came to Burford, which is distant from Oxford about sixteen miles. There we refreshed ourselves awhile, and his Majesty was so graciously disposed that he would have my father and me to sup with him and the great lords that were about his person. After supper he talked with my father awhile about military affairs, asking his opinion in the most courteous fashion; and he had also a few words with me about my books, not forgetting to warn me that I must not neglect them for any pleasures or excitements of war. About nine of the clock the King, desiring to put as much space as might be between himself and his pursuers, gave command to march, which was performed, but not without some murmuring. And, indeed, it was a laborious march, for though our way for the most part lay along the valley, yet at the last, it being little short of midnight, we made a steep ascent, and so having mounted the height with no small pains, descended the same with no less to Bourton-on-the-Water. Here we rested for the night, keeping under such shelter as we could find, or, the greater part of us, under none at all. We had marched, I take it, not less than thirty miles, which is no small achievement, especially for an army that had been for many months past in garrison. The next day betimes we set forth again, the King intending at the first to halt at Evesham, but after hearing that General Waller was in pursuit, and that crossing the Avon at Stratford might so cut him off from Worcester, to which place he was bound, changed his purpose and went on without halt to Worcester. And here I must record a marvellous deliverance from instant danger that befell me on my way. 'Twas at Pershore in Worcestershire, where there is a bridge over the Avon. This the King commanded should be broken down, and gave commandment accordingly to the officer that had the charge of such matters. But he being either new to his business, or overhasty to finish the matter, lest the enemy should perchance come up and find it undone, set fire to the gunpowder wherewith it was to be destroyed, before the due time. By this misadventure Major Bridges, a very skilful and courageous man, was killed, and with him also three other officers and about twenty common soldiers. I myself was like to have perished with these, being thrown into the river, by the falling of the bridge. But being somewhat before the others I escaped, for whereas they were done to death by the force of the explosion, I did but lose my footing and fall into the river. And here again my good steed showed how excellent a beast he was, for he swam most bravely against the stream, and in the end landed me on the bank, being not much the worse, save for the wetting. From Evesham the King rode to Worcester, where the townsfolk received him with much rejoicing.

CHAPTER VII.

OF THE FIGHT AT COPREDY BRIDGE.

OF his Majesty's marchings and countermarchings, after his coming to the City of Worcester, I shall not write in this place, save to say that they were ordered with such skill as utterly confounded his pursuers. But they that read this book will, I doubt not, pardon me if I speak somewhat particularly of the battle which his Majesty fought at Copredy Bridge, seeing that it was the first battle in which I had a hand.

On the twenty-eighth day of June, being a Friday, the army lay for the night in the field, eastward of Banbury. The next day the King marched to the North, having the Cherwell River on his left hand, Sir William Waller at the same time coasting on the other side of the river. My father and I were with the rear of the army, in which were a thousand foot and two brigades of horse of which the one was commanded by my Lord Northampton, and the other by my Lord Cleveland. In this latter was the regiment of which my father had charge for the time. About noon we halted to dine. This business finished, we began again to march, not expecting that the enemy, who was some way distant from the river, would fall upon us. But about two of the clock we noted that the body of the army—with which was the King himself—had since dinner made such haste that there was now a great space left between them and us; for we had received no command to quicken our marching. Being somewhat uneasy at this—for it was not to be doubted that Sir William Waller, being a man experienced in warfare, would take occasion of this dividing of the army to fall upon us—we spied certain scattered horsemen riding towards us, with such hurry and confusion as men are when they are pursued. While we wondered what this might mean comes a rider post-haste to my Lord Cleveland, and says:

"My Lord, be on your guard, and make

ready to defend yourselves. The enemy has taken Copredy Bridge, which the Dragoons were keeping for the King, and will cross the river in a short space of time. 'Tis said that he has five thousand men and twenty pieces of cannon."

These numbers were exaggerated by fame, as is commonly the case, for there were, in truth, little more than half the number. At the same time, we perceived that a brigade of horse, which we reckoned at about a thousand, had crossed the river by a certain ford, which was a mile below the bridge, and was ready to fall upon us in the rear. These latter, being the nearer to us of the two, seemed to my Lord Cleveland to demand his first care. Thereupon he drew up his brigade to a rising ground, which faced the ford aforesaid, and passed the word that we should make ready to charge. Then we all descended from our horses and looked to our saddle-girths, that they should not fail us, and to the trimming of our pistols. Then, mounting again, we drew our swords, and so sat waiting for the word. Whether during that said waiting I felt any fear I can scarce say.

'Tis, indeed, a mighty difficult thing clearly to distinguish between fear and other feelings that are somewhat akin to it. The Latins had a certain word—*trepidare*, to wit—which has a singular variety of meaning. That it has something to do with "trembling" there can scarce be doubt, and it does often signify such agitation of mind as is commonly shown by trembling; yet sometimes also its meaning seems to be "haste" only; and, indeed, a man may tremble for eagerness and not for fear. That I had any thought of flying or shrinking back I can, with a good conscience, deny. A man must be beside himself with fear that should think of such a thing; but my heart beat mighty quick, and I thought of them that were dear to me as might one who thinks to see them no more. While these things were in my mind comes my father, riding along in front of the line, to see that all were ready. When he comes to me—I being placed at the right end of the line—he laid his right hand on my shoulder, and said, "Be steady, son Philip; let not your horse carry you too fast. That you be not too slow I need not warn you." ('Twas marvellous what heart he put into me by these words, which seemed to take my courage as something beyond doubt.) "Give the point of your sword to an enemy rather than the edge, and keep your pistols for a last resource, when you shalt find yourself in close quarters with an enemy and like to be hard pressed."

When he had said so much the trumpet sounded for a charge, and we set spurs to our horses, and rode, slowly at the first, and keeping our ranks passably well, but afterwards at our horses' full speed, and in a certain disorder. I do believe that the veriest coward upon earth could not fear if he once found himself riding in a charge; a man cannot choose but forget himself, and, if he have no courage of his own, he takes that of his company and is content to meet dangers at which he would otherwise tremble and grow pale. The enemy had scarce finished their crossing of the river; and though they put on a bold face, and even began to move forward to encounter us, they could not stand, but were broken at the first encounter. For myself, I clean forgot my father's command that

I should give the point of my sword, and struck lustily, often missing my blow altogether, and doing but little at other times but blunting my sword. 'Twas all the better so for one of the enemy's horse that was overthrown by our charge. He was a lad of seventeen or thereabouts, a brave youth, for he would stand his ground though his men left him. But now he and his horse went down before us, and that straight in my way. Thereupon, being on the ground and helpless, he cried "Quarter!" Now, whether or no I heard him is more than I can say, but I must confess with shame that I was so carried out of myself with the fury of battle that it was as if he had not spoken, for I struck at him, so lying, with all my might. But the fury which caused me so to forget myself did also make me altogether miss my aim. God be thanked therefor! for otherwise that day had been to me for all my life such a shame and sorrow as cannot be expressed. As I was in the act to lift my sword again—for I will conceal nothing—I felt a hand upon my arm that held it as with a grip of iron; and my father, for it was he, cried in such a voice as I had never before heard from his lips, "What savage is that that will slay a Christian man when he cries 'Quarter'?" Thereat I dropped my sword, being, so to speak, come to myself, and mightily ashamed. My father leapt down from his horse, and said to the young man, "Yield yourself to me, and you shall suffer no harm." Then the young man, who, now that I had leisure, I could see to be a cornet, yielded up his sword, and my father bade one of the troopers take him to the rear. This done, he turned him to me and said, "I had almost as lief you were a coward as a madman. Be you one or the other, this is not fit place for you, and you had better depart."

"Nay, my father," I said, "disgrace me not. I will hold myself in better check hereafter."

By this time the enemy had fallen back on their supports, and my Lord Cleveland sounded the bugle, and we rode back slowly to our former place. There was, I remember, a great ash-tree there, under which the King stayed to take his dinner. Looking about him there, my Lord saw another body of the enemy within musket shot of him and advancing upon him (these were the Parliament men that had come over the bridge). I doubt not but that in any case he would have charged them, though they counted sixteen cornets of horse and as many colours of foot, but now he was the more encouraged, because he saw that the body of the King's army was drawing to his help. When the enemy saw him move forwards, they halted, hiding behind the hedges, and delivered their volley of musket and carbine shot, which volley, though it emptied some of our saddles, stayed not our charge. Indeed, they did not abide our approach (and, indeed, I have noted that for the most part there is but little crossing of swords or pikes in battle, but they that give place yield to the persuasion of superior force that they conceive in their minds), but we drave them, with scarce a blow struck, beyond their cannon. These also we took, being eleven in number, and besides the cannon two barricadoes of wood drawn up on wheels; in each of these were seven small guns of brass and leather, loaded with case-shot, which, by God's mercy, they had not tarried to discharge; else, I doubt

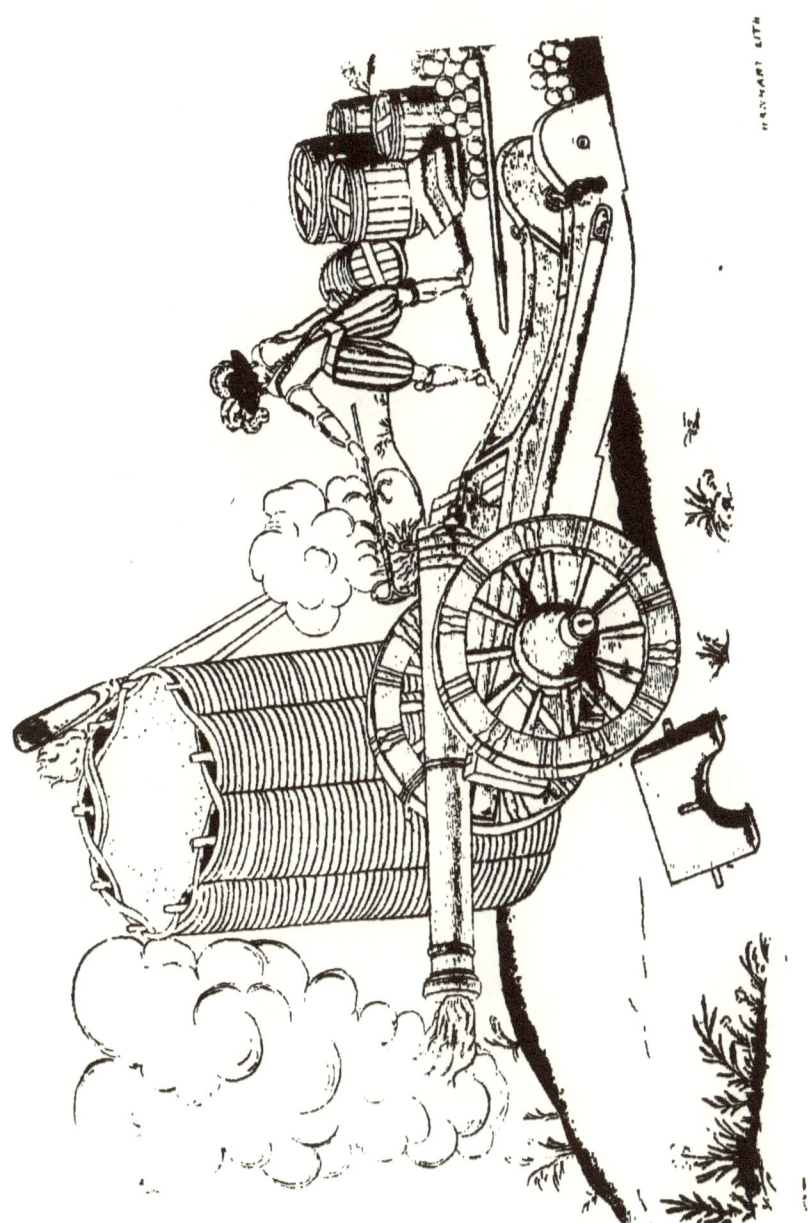

A Gunner.

OF THE FIGHT AT COPREDY BRIDGE. 89

not, we had suffered much damage. Certain of the cannoneers were killed, and the general of the ordnance taken prisoner. This was a certain Scotsman, by name Wemyss, who was in very ill favour with the King's men, because, having been made master-gunner of England, with a very considerable pension, to the prejudice of many honest Englishmen, he took the first opportunity to do him hurt. Many other prisoners were taken, nearly two hundred in all. In this charge I bore myself more discreetly, riding as close as I could to my father, but I found no occasion to cross swords with any enemy, for here again they did not abide our charge, but turned when we were about a pistol-shot from them. As for them that were slain, who were in number more than the prisoners, they fell in the flight, for the most part without striking a blow, though some parties of them rallied and fought for their lives. Of our party there fell, chiefly in this way, somewhat less than a score, among whom were two colonels of regiments.

Here was finished my part in this battle. Of what else was done that day little needs to be said. The horsemen that crossed by the ford, making head again and threatening our rear, were charged by my Lord Northampton, and driven across the river; indeed, these stayed not at all my Lord's approach, but fled so speedily and so far that 'tis said they never returned again to their own army.

So far things went altogether well for the King. But when his Majesty would himself attack the enemy he fared not so well. The bridge he could not take for all his endeavours, which he continued from three of the clock in the afternoon till nightfall; and though his men took the ford that was below and a mill adjoining thereto, and held them that day and the next also, not being supported by their fellows, they were compelled to retire. 'Tis beyond doubt, however, that the victory rested with the King; for though when the battle was finished each party held the same ground that it had at the first, yet the enemy lost many times more both in killed and prisoners. Nor must it be forgotten, as showing what the rebels themselves did think of the matter, that whereas Sir William Waller on the day of the battle had

OF THE FIGHT AT COPREDY BRIDGE. 91

eight thousand men with him, fourteen days afterward there remained with him not half that number.

The next day the cornet of horse whom my father had taken prisoner was exchanged. It was his good fortune that on our side also there had been taken an officer of the same degree. He was a lad of sixteen or thereabouts, somewhat weakly of body, though of a very high spirit, and was carried by his horse, which he could not by any means restrain, into the midst of the enemy. As for the colonels and others of high degree, they had to wait, there not being any of ours who could be exchanged against them. We had some talk with the lad while we lay encamped that night on the field of battle, but he held back and would say but little. But this much I gathered from him, that he had gone to the wars without the consent of his father. At the same time he was very hot about certain wrongs which his father had suffered from the King or the King's Ministers, though what they were he did not more particularly set forth. He told me that he came from Northamptonshire, and that his father had purposed to send him to

Lincoln College, in which this county, as belonging to the diocese of Oxford, has with others a certain preference.

On the last day of June I returned to Oxford, my father remaining with the King, who was minded to march westward.

CHAPTER VIII.

OF THE PLAGUE AT OXFORD AND OTHER MATTERS.

THE members of Lincoln College were for the most part inclined to the Parliament, though the King had also some friends among them. The chief of these was one Master Webberley, a Fellow, a man of a litigious and disputatious temper, whom his Majesty's cause doubtless pleased the better that it pleased not the greater part of his society. But 'twould be ungracious in me to speak ill of him, not only because he always showed me much kindness, but because he was content, as will be seen hereafter, to suffer for his opinions. As for Doctor Hood, the Rector, he was, as I have said, somewhat of a weathercock, turning always according to the wind that blew. Now, on my coming back to my chamber, he was mighty pleasant to me (chancing to meet me in the new quadrangle) and told me that the College was proud to have one who could use both his sword and pen, and other fine things of the same kind, which there is no need to report. 'Twas fair weather then with the King's cause, but 'twas clouded over very soon, and Master Rector's countenance changed therewith. It was not four days afterwards that he passed me, taking no heed of my reverence which before he had most courteously acknowledged. Then thought I with myself, "Doubtless, there is ill news from the King." And so it was, as I heard within the space of half-an-hour, viz., that the Prince Rupert and my Lord Newcastle (but my Lord Newcastle was in no ways to blame, as I have heard) had suffered a most grievous defeat at Marston Moor, near to the City of York, at which defeat well nigh the whole of the north country was lost to the King. From that day I had small favour from Master Rector. But with this I concerned myself but little.

During the vacation, that is about the space of three months and more, from July to October, I applied myself diligently to my books, though

I did not neglect my military exercises; in them I was by this time somewhat proficient. Indeed, as having done actual service in war I had an officer's place amongst the troop which was raised by the University for the King, and myself taught the rudiments of the military art to the new comers. And, indeed, there was but little recreation other than soldiering. There was much playing, indeed, with cards and dice in the guard-houses, but such things were never to my taste, nor indeed had I the gold pieces which are a man's best introduction to such places. But as for the sport that was followed outside the walls, fishing and fowling, to wit, and the like enjoyments, it was hardly to be got. It was as like as not that he who went forth hoping to catch something should himself be caught. I do not call to mind indeed that I had any sport, save only fives play with a certain Edward Wood, second son of Mistress Wood, of whom, as I have written above, my father rented a house in Oxford. The said Edward Wood was a portionist, or, as it is sometimes named, a postmaster, of Merton College, and we were wont to use the fives play in the garden, that lies on the south side of the chapel of the said College. At the west end of this garden the wall has been built up higher than ordinary to serve this purpose, and the grass has been exchanged for stone. Sometimes one or other of the young courtiers would join us at our play. I know not whether I had pleasanter times than in this fives court. Edward Wood did not tarry long at Merton College, being promoted to a scholarship at Trinity College, but I was privileged to use the place till the very end of my sojourn in Oxford.

At the beginning of the next term there fell upon the City of Oxford a dreadful calamity, that is to say, a fire, so great as had not been known within the memory of living man. It is said, indeed, that, considering the shortness of the time wherein it burned, it exceeded in damage all fires that had before been in England. It began on Sunday, the eighth day of October, about two of the clock in the afternoon in a little poor house on the south side of Thames Street (which leads from the North Gate to the East Bridge). The wind blew from the north,

Merton College Chapel. Fives-play in the Garden.

and being very high greatly increased the damage, so that much of the city that was built to the south of Thames Street was consumed. On the other hand it is to be remembered that no hall, or college, or church, or magazine for ammunition or victuals, was consumed. As for the cause of this conflagration, there was much diversity of opinion. It was to be expected that it should be laid to the account of the Parliament soldiers, of whom there was a body at Abingdon town, not more than three miles distant from Oxford. Indeed, one of their officers, a Major Burne by name, had, it was said, threatened this very thing against the city. He was reported to have cried out, "If I cannot burn all Oxford, yet will I burn so much as I can." It was allowed also that the fire burst out in many places at once, and it could not therefore have been caused by an accident. Also the time of its breaking out was noted, which was two of the clock in the afternoon, when many of the citizens were at church, and so unable to attend to the speedy putting out of the flames. For myself I take little heed of these things, which would in any case have been said. On the other hand it is certain that the fire in the house in Thames Street came from a footsoldier roasting a pig which he had stolen. Of the buildings that were consumed the most important were a printing-office and a house which had been newly set apart for the keeping of wills.

The next year—to speak of calamities which befell the city—when the summer began to draw on, there befell a great sickness of the plague. It may be said that during the whole time, from the King's first coming to Oxford to the surrender of the city, the distemper never altogether departed, seeming to sleep during the cold weather, but waking again and raging, now less, now more, when the spring returned. Nor was this to be wondered at. For it was with Oxford as it was with the City of Athens in the Peloponnesian War, of which Thucydides has written. 'Twas grievously overcrowded; for there lodged therein the King and his Court and officers of the Government and the army, to the number, not always, indeed, but sometimes, of ten thousand and more, and many traders that came thither for the sake of trading, buying, and selling, and not a few of the

OF THE PLAGUE AT OXFORD.

King's party that sought shelter within the walls, as indeed did my mother and sister. Of scholars, indeed there were but few, the University being then changed into a garrison town. Nevertheless, the number of souls in the city must have been doubled and more; and these also confined within a very narrow space, for it was not possible to live without the walls for fear of the enemy.

About April, therefore, in this year (which is the year 1645), the plague beginning to increase, the Councillor of the city issued a proclamation concerning it. If any house was suspected of the plague it was commanded to be shut up, and all the persons within it commanded to be kept in the house till orders should be given for opening of it again. Also the house was to be marked with a red cross, and "THE LORD HAVE MERCY UPON US" writ in capital letters. And to each house so shut up there was appointed a watchman to see that none went in or out, and to fetch such necessaries as they might have need of. These watchmen carried a white staff, and took an oath that they would perform their duty faithfully. It was not an office to be desired, but if a man was elected thereto he had no choice but to take it. But the most dreadful thing in this visitation was the order that was kept concerning the burial of the dead. There went carts about ('tis a most surprising thing that they who drove the carts and they who fetched the dead bodies out of the houses, for the most part, escaped the disease), after ten of the clock at night, and carried away the corpses of such as had died during the day. Nor was it permitted that these should be buried in the churchyards of the city, but great pits were dug in such places as could be found that were farthest removed from the habitations of man. There were the dead heaped together, without coffin, ay, and often without shroud, and after a service, which a chaplain would make as short and say as speedily as he could, so left. I know not whether the war brought any worse horror than this.

In the colleges none, I think, were affected, none certainly perished. But in those parts of the town that lie by the river where the poorer sort do dwell many died. Yet the mortality was never so great that there prevailed any great and general terror. The ministers of religion also, and the physicians, of whom there was then in Oxford a greater number than ordinary, did not desert their places; and it is always, I have heard, to be noted that where these are steadfast to their duty, they infect others, if I may so speak, with their courage, to the great advantage of the whole state. But whether they that were stricken by this sickness profited much by the help of the physicians is somewhat to be doubted. I have it from one who has had much experience of the plague, both here and in foreign parts, especially among the Turks, where it is to be found almost every year, that the course of the distemper is such that at its first coming the aid of the physicians can recover none, or at the best very few; and that when its first violence is spent, 'tis an even chance with them; and that afterwards, 'tis but very few that die under their hands. It is certainly true that they would use a great variety of remedies, from which may be gathered that such as prospered under their hands were saved by Nature rather than by art. Of these remedies one was sold much among the people, but the men of science made but small account of it. It was said to have been given to King Henry VIII. by a very learned physician of his time. For curiosity's sake I have here written it down.

A handful of elder leaves; a handful of red bramble leaves. Stamp and strain them through a fine cloth with a quart of white wine; then take a quantity of ginger. Mingle these together, and take a spoonful of the mixture, and you shall be safe for twenty-four days.

This then was the prophylactic; but the remedy was this:

The water of Scabius, a spoonful; the water of Betany, a spoonful; of fine treacle, a quantity. This shall put out the venom, by the grace of God.

The last clause does save it, to my mind. "The grace of God" can give potency to plain water. Indeed, I know not whether there be anything that is to be preferred to this. So at least some of the wise men will have it.

There needed not indeed either fire or plague to make all hearts dull and cheerless; all, I should say, that were well disposed to the King, for he had enemies even here. Of all the gaiety and show that had adorned the city after his

Majesty's first coming there was but little left. The Queen and her ladies had departed to Exeter, in which city was born, in this same year, the Princess Henrietta. Of the nobles and gentlemen that had come with the King, or flowed to him afterwards, many were dead, for his Majesty was most unfortunate in the loss of friends; many had been taken prisoners, and they that remained were sadly shorn of their means. Hence it was but the name and shadow of a Court that surrounded the King; of its pomp and glory, its splendour and riches, nothing was left. To the colleges little remained save that which could not be alienated. Their plate they had given up to the King's service, and it was now melted into money which had long since been spent; in some places the very libraries were dissipated. As for learning, its voice was well nigh silenced. The very schools had passed from their original use, and were filled with stores of ammunition and arms. Over everything there hung the cloud of ill-fortune and ill-success. 'Twas a University to which none came to learn (I do suppose that from the time at which I came to Oxford till the surrender of the city there were matriculated, that is to say, entered the University, scarce two score), and a Court that lacked both power and magnificence, and a camp from which had departed all hope of victory.

When this year (I speak of the year academical, which runs from October to July) was drawing to an end there happened great events, great both for the nation and for me, of which I will now proceed to write.

CHAPTER IX.

BEFORE NASEBY.

SITTING in my chamber in the month of June, in the year 1645—I remember that it was St. Barnabas' Day, and that Master Chalfont, who was Sub-Rector of Lincoln College, had preached that morning at St. Mary's Church —comes a knock at my outer door, which I had shut, fearing hindrances to my study; for in those days there was scarce a place in the whole kingdom less given to study than Oxford. At the first I heeded it not; for what would it have profited, having shut the door, to open it on the first occasion? But when the knocking grew more urgent I called through the door, "Who knocks?" to which came an answer in a voice that I seemed to know, "Open, Master Philip, 'tis an urgent matter." When I heard this "Master Philip," I understood that the voice was of John Talboys, that was a trooper in my father's regiment, and born, too, of a family that had been servants, ay, and friends, to ours for many generations, and was in great trust with him. So I opened the door in no small trepidation; but when I saw the good fellow's face I knew that it was no ill-tidings that he brought. "What news, John, from the army? How fares it with my father?"

"Your father was well when I left him yesterday morning: but take this letter; it will tell you more than any words of mine."

So I took the letter, which was written on a scrap of paper about the bigness of a mulberry leaf, for the convenience of hiding if occasion arose; or, it might be, of swallowing, if the hiding could not be otherwise contrived. It ran thus:

"*My dear son Philip,—It irks me much to draw you away yet again from your studies, yet it is, to my mind, a plain necessity so to do. Hear now the cause, which I will put as shortly as it is possible, lest, haply, this writing should fall under less friendly eyes than yours. 'Tis plain to me, from signs that I see, that a great battle will be fought within a few days, by which the King's cause shall be made or marred; and I hold that every man who can strike a blow for his sacred Majesty, and is not kept away by some necessity, should be here to do his duty. Of myself*

I speak not, save only that I would fain have you with me. Do all your diligence, then, to come. John Talboys, the bearer of this epistle, and not unknown to you, will be your guide. God keep you.

"*Your loving Father,*

"*Philip Dashwood.*

"*Writ at Daintree, in the county of Northampton, the tenth day of June, at four of the clock before noon.*"

"Well, John," I said, when I had read this letter, "What say you to all this? But stay"—for when I looked at him I saw that he was pale and weary, and, had he been less stalwart and strong, almost like to faint—"speak not till I fetch you somewhat."

With that I ran out of College and fetched in a flagon of ale and a manchet of bread, with some cheese, from the *Maidenhead* tavern, for the buttery was not yet open, it being not yet noon. It was against law to fetch such things from without, and I was commonly law-abiding, but the need was urgent. Therefore, I hesitated not to transgress, and to hide my transgression also under my academic habiliments, the scholars' gown having full sleeves that are not ill-contrived on occasion to conceal a flagon or the like.

I perceived John's eyes glitter when he saw

the meat and drink ; and when he had taken a deep draught of the ale, and a few mouthfuls of the bread, he said :

"This is right welcome, Master Philip. I have not had bit nor sup since I left the King's army at Daintree yesterday morning about five of the clock, save only a crust of bread which a good parson gave me at Banbury yesterday evening. The good man had nothing better for himself, for the Parliament men had stripped him bare. I know not when I have tasted better ale than this."

But this was John's fancy, bred, I take it, of his long fasting. It was but poor drink, and nothing to be compared with that of our own buttery.

"And now, sir," he went on, "for business. My good master, the Colonel, wants you to bear him company. He read me the letter after he had written it, so that if there came occasion to destroy the paper I might give its substance by word of mouth. It is not the easiest thing in the world to make our way hence to the King; but I have a good hope that we shall. I know every by-road and hiding-place in the country, and 'tis hard if I contrive not to give the slip to these crop-eared psalm-singing gentry. I must needs give my horse a rest, and you will need some time for your making yourself ready. What say you to ten of the clock this night for our setting out? We shall pass the worst of the country while it is still dark."

"But tell me, John," I said; "is it going well with the King?"

"'Tis not," he answered, "for a common man to speak; but, as you ask, I will say that I like not the aspect of affairs. We have men, though not so many as they; the gentlefolk are mostly with us, but the commonalty are greatly against us. But 'tis counsel that we chiefly lack. The Prince Rupert is in great authority; and as he has lost us already one battle, so, I misdoubt me, he will lose us another. And I hear of one Cromwell, a brewer by trade, they say, that is a mighty dangerous enemy. It was he that turned the battle against the King at Marston Moor, and, if I err not, we shall hear of him again. And now I will get some sleep, if I can, and at ten of the clock to-night, at the North Gate, I shall reckon to see you."

I had little preparation to make. Leave of absence from the Rector I judged it better to take rather than to ask. My good beast Spot was, I knew, at my service when I should need him, for it had been so arranged, and my accoutrements I kept, not in my chamber at College, but at the tavern where Spot was stabled. So, after I had seen that my horse and arms should be ready for me at the time appointed, I had little else to do than make my farewells to my friends. First I went to Master Webberley, who was, as I have said, well affected to the King, and told him my purpose. Of this he greatly approved, and gave me his blessing, and, as a token of his good will, a flask of sherry sack. We agreed that when inquiry of my absence should be made, he should answer that I had been called away by an urgent demand from my father that would not brook delay. It fell out by great good-luck that for the day there was none other Fellow within the College but Master Webberley, the others having gone to see an estate that the College possesses near to this city. Nor did I go back to the College after taking leave of him, fearing lest some one should stay me and ask questions, but passed the remainder of the day with my mother and sister. My dear mother was sorely divided between two desires; for while she would gladly have kept me with her, she did also greatly wish that I should be with my father, believing that we should be safer together. Yet, though she was convinced of this, and, indeed, reckoned the chance higher than it deserved, yet it troubled her much to think that we should both be running into the same danger at the same time. Her poor heart was sadly distracted this way and that. This is the unhappiness of women that they have ever a choice, though, indeed, it is a choice but in name only, between evils of which they cannot say which is the more to be dreaded or the worse to bear. My mother gave me many messages, and would have laden me and my horse beyond all possibility of moving with good things, an I had not refused them. She seemed to think that I had a waggon at the least to follow me, carrying what I might want. I remember her great concern when I told her that I should sleep on the ground in my cloak. She was urgent with me that I should take a mattress with me, and would have given me one off her own bed. I had no small difficulty to persuade her that the thing was impossible. After that I was content to tell her something less than the whole truth about our life in the camp; for she followed me beyond the door, bidding me never to put on clean linen that had not been first aired at the fire.

It favoured us much that the night was dark as could well be at midsummer, with such a roaring of the wind, which was more than commonly stormy for that season of the year, that the noise of our horses' hoofs could scarcely have been heard at twenty yards' distance. We journeyed, too, by green lanes and by-ways, which John Talboys knew marvellously well, rather than by high roads. Nevertheless, we did not draw rein, save for a few minutes' breathing space, till we came to Brackley, which is a small market town in the county of Northampton, lying south by west of Banbury. We halted about half-a-mile short of the town, where was a farmhouse that had been deserted during the present troubles. We bestowed ourselves and our horses in a barn, and laid ourselves down to sleep, Talboys first taking some whiffs of tobacco, a herb in which he professes to find much comfort. "Trouble not yourself, Master Philip," he said, before he slept, "to wake over early; for we must be content to pass the day here, and that without company, if we would not fall into the hands of our enemies." I verily believe that it was noon before I awoke; for I was much wearied by my ride, having been pent up in the city for nearly a twelvemonth, and my legs never once across a horse's back.

I had just roused myself, and was looking about me, half-dazed, as a man will sometimes be with a long slumber, when I heard a whistle, to which straightway John whistles an answer. Thereupon an old man thrusts his head in at the door, and presently follows with his whole body. He was a parson, a man, I should say, of sixty or thereabouts, his hair quite white, his face ruddy, with as merry a look in his eyes as ever man had. He had a priest's cloak on him, which he threw off so soon as he came within the door.

"Now beshrew this cloak," he said, with a laugh; "'tis cumbrous wear for a midsummer day; but 'tis a rare thing if one has ought to hide; better than a college gown; eh, Master Scholar?" Then we saw that he had something in his hand wrapped in a napkin, which, when he had unfolded, we saw a roasted capon.

"Ah!" he said; "if the King had had such politicians about him as I am, he had been better served. Hear now how you have come by your dinner. My good housekeeper, Dorothy Leggats, serves me up this capon, one of a couple that a neighbour brought me yesterday. Now an I had told her that I needed it for you, first there would have been loud complainings, for the good woman believes in her heart that I starve myself; then she would have gone 'clack, clack' over the whole village, for the good woman can no more keep a secret than a sieve can hold water. So, says I, rubbing my hands; 'That is a goodly sight for a hungry man, Dorothy, but I have business on hand, affairs of State, you understand, and I must not be disturbed for three hours at the least. So if anyone come you must say that the parson has shut himself in his chamber, and cannot be spoken with.' So I lock the door on her, and slip out of the window, which, by good fortune, is near the road, and here I am."

"We thank you much, sir;" I said, "but where shall you get your own dinner?"

"Nay," answered the good man, "let me care for that. 'Tis little that I can do for his Majesty, and I should be a bad subject if I should think of myself when there are two stout soldiers in need, that can strike a blow for him, which my cloth forbids me to do. I shall make my Friday fast to-day, and give myself indulgence for flesh and fowl, if such fall in my way, when Friday itself shall come."

"Ah! Master Parson," said John, "I reckon that you fast on other days than Friday. But come, take a morsel with us; for there is more than enough for us two."

We had some trouble to persuade him; but at the last he consented to share with us; and a right jovial meal we had, though we had nothing stronger to drink than a pitcher of water that John had drawn from the well in the farmyard the night before. The good parson stayed talking with us till, as he said, his time was out. He had been at Oxford, at St. John's College, about forty years before, when the Archbishop of Canterbury whom the Parliament so barbarously put to death, was his tutor. Of him he had many things to say, of which I will here set down one. "They did him an ill turn that brought him to Court, and put him in the way of preferment and of office in the State. It had been well for him as for the realm also if he had had no higher place than to be president of his college. Learning never had a more duteous son nor the King a worse counsellor."

When it was time for the good man to go he was much concerned to part from us. "Were I ten years younger," said he, "I would ride with you, cloth or no cloth. There are days when it may be said, 'Let him that hath no sword sell his cloak and buy one,' though, to speak the truth, I could not buy much with this of mine, so threadbare is it and ragged. But an old man like me is best at home; I can pray for his Majesty in the church so long as they suffer me to keep it, and when they turn me out, if they extinguish my voice, still my thoughts will be free. And now, my sons, take my blessing."

So he blessed us and went his way. We two lay hiding till it grew dark, and then setting out arrived without misadventure at Burrough Hill, where the King lay. We saw the light of Sir Thomas Fairfax's camp at Kislingbury on our right hand, and once were constrained to hide ourselves in a thicket, so near came some of the enemy's horsemen. But scarce had we come to his Majesty's camp ('twas about four of the clock in the morning) when there comes an order that the army should march, the King proposing to go towards Newark, where he had a strong garrison, with whom, as with other forces which he expected, he could strengthen himself. It had been well had he done so! So accordingly we set fire to the huts and departed, making a short stage to Market Harborough, where we rested that night, that is to say the van of the army, for the rear was at Naseby, his Majesty himself sleeping at Lubbenham, which lies between the two. I had gone to bed betimes, being not a little wearied with my journey, having ridden two nights. (It is commonly thought among soldiers that journeying will weary a man by night more than by day, for all that he may so shun the heat, it being against nature to wake at such hours.) I had scarce slept an hour (to me it seemed but five minutes, so weary was I with sleep) when there comes an alarm, the rear coming in with no small confusion from Naseby, where the Parliament men had suddenly fallen upon them, and, taking some prisoners, had driven the rest northward. I perceived that there was small hope of sleep that night, and so rose and made ready for what might happen. I was quartered with my father (whom his Majesty would always have near him) in a house in the village, and coming out into the street, saw the King set out for Harborough, where the Prince Rupert lay, my father riding with him in the carriage. This was about an hour before midnight. In the space of three hours or thereabouts my father comes back. There was a cloud upon his face, and I could see that he was ill-pleased. "We are resolved to fight," says he, "and 'twill be a marvel if we are not well beaten. I was at the Council by his Majesty's favour, and heard the debate, though it did not become one of my station to thrust in my voice. The greater part were urgent for battle, the Prince being especially vehement. Reason for fighting heard I none from him or from any other; but his Highness's pride was affronted because the Parliament men had fallen upon the King's army. They must teach the Roundheads, forsooth, to bear themselves more modestly, as if that was good reason for putting the whole future of the realm upon the cast of a die. For 'tis nothing less than that, son Philip. If we be beaten to-day, and I fear much that we shall, there is an end to the King's cause. The King was for delay and gathering his forces together, but was overborne, and gave way, as indeed it is too much his failing to do, to these hot-blooded youngsters, who think that war is but a matter of hard blows. But come, we must be moving; the army is to be drawn together about a mile south from Harborough."

CHAPTER X.

OF NASEBY FIGHT.

It was about five of the clock in the morning on Saturday, the 14th day of June, that the drawing up of the King's army was finished. In the centre was my Lord Astley with about two thousand five hundred foot; on the right the Prince Rupert with about two thousand horse; and on the left Sir Marmaduke Langdale with the northern horse, about sixteen hundred in all. In the reserves were about thirteen hundred, horse and foot together; so that there were in all scarce eight thousand, the horse and foot being well nigh equal in number.

About eight of the clock in the morning comes a rumour that the enemy had retired. Thereupon the scout-master is sent out, and certain horsemen with him, among whom was John Talboys and I, to make further discovery. We rode about two miles and a half, or, it may be three, and saw nothing. Then said the scout-master: "This report is manifestly true; these rascals are in great fear of us, and have fled." Thereupon he turned back with his company to carry the tidings to the King. Then says John Talboys to me: "I take it Master Scout-master has scarce gone far enough. Do you see yonder height? What say you to going thither? If we can see nothing there, then 'tis plain that they are indeed gone."

We rode as he had said, and no sooner were we gotten to the top of the hill than we saw the enemy almost under our feet. So close were we to them that a gunner aimed a small cannon that he had at us, and we could hear the bullet pass over our heads. "We have seen enough," says John; "let us go back."

Thereupon we galloped back, and found that the Prince had moved forward some horsemen and musqueteers, as thinking that the report of the enemy's retreat, which, indeed, had been in some sort confirmed by the scout-master, was true. We told him what we had seen, but he seemed to be persuaded in his mind that the enemy were now retreating. So he says to me: "Ride to my Lord Astley and tell him to come forward with all the haste he can, if he would not have the enemy escape us; and you," he said, turning to John Talboys, "carry the same words to Sir Marmaduke." It was not for me to question his bidding, so I rode with all the speed I could, and delivered the message to my Lord Astley, who, nothing questioning, for the Prince being in the van could not but know the truth, gave orders to advance with all speed.

When we came to the hill-top (the same at which the scout-master had halted) we saw, I being in the following of my Lord Astley, the Prince Rupert in the level ground below us, and on the brow of the hill beyond, to which John Talboys and I had ridden, the army of the Parliament. These last drew back so soon as we came into their view—it was but a hundred yards or so—the better to hide themselves and their plans; but we, or at the least some of us, imagined that they fled. Thereupon we moved on the faster, so fast indeed that we left behind much of our ordnance. Indeed, it is scarce to be believed how all through the day we continually put ourselves at a disadvantage.

A Cavalry Skirmish.

The Prince Rupert began the battle, charging the enemy's left wing. I saw him and his horsemen gallop up the slope of the hill past some thick hedges, from which came forth a fire of musketry (the hedges being lined with dragoons on foot) which emptied some saddles, yet not so many as to check them. More of the Prince's doings I could not see, he passing from our view when he had got to the brow of the hill; but I heard that he broke the enemy's left wing, scattering them all ways, and then rode on as if he would have taken the baggage. 'Tis said that the captain of the baggage guard took him for Sir Thomas Fairfax, he wearing a red Spanish cloak after his lordship's fashion, and went to him, hat in hand, and asked: "How goes the day?" thinking that he was the General; and that thereupon the Prince asked whether they would have quarter, which they refused, and gave him a volley instead, which beat him and his horsemen off. On the other wing the Parliament men did not wait for our coming but charged Sir Marmaduke Langdale's horse, taking advantage of the ground, and to such a purpose that, after some smart blows given and taken, our horsemen were beaten off, and, indeed, fought no more that day.

Nevertheless, it seemed for a while as if the day would go well for us, for the main body of our foot charging against the main body of theirs did great execution upon them. The lines fired but one volley upon each other, nor did either do much damage, aiming too high, as young soldiers are wont to do, and then came to swords and the butt ends of their muskets. I do protest that however much I might be minded to magnify myself and my deeds, I could by no means tell what I did that day. I know only this that I found my sword somewhat hacked and some shrewd cuts in my buff-coat, but wound had I none save a bruise upon the forepart of the left shoulder from a musket bullet that by great happiness had spent itself before ever it came near to me. But altogether we used our swords and muskets to such good purpose that the enemy fled, though the officers for the most part, and especially they that had the colours, stood bravely to their posts. The victory being, as we judged, thus assured, my Lord Astley bethought him whether he could not succour the left wing, which the King also, who was with his guards in the reserve, was making ready to support in their need. Whereupon he sends me with this message to the King: "Does your Majesty need help?" This I was on the point to deliver, his Majesty being at the head of his guards, and preparing to charge, when I saw my Lord Carnworth, who was riding next to the King, lay his hand upon his bridle, the next moment my Lord cried out with a great oath: "Will you go upon your death in an instant?" and so saying, turned the King's horse round. After this the command was given: "March to the right." Now this marching to the right led them away both from helping their own and from charging the enemy. In whose voice it was given I cannot affirm, but 'tis certain that it was too readily obeyed. When my father, who was setting the second line of the guards in order, saw what was doing, he rode with all the speed of his horse to the King and said: "Pardon me, sir, but it is ruin absolute if we leave the field in this fashion." Then the King, who here again had yielded against his will and better judgment to the worse counsel, cried with a loud voice: "Stand." But, though some obeyed this command, yet for the greater part it was too late. Almost at the instant of the King's speaking came a musket shot from the enemy's ranks and wounded my father, entering by the left arm, which it broke, and lodging in his shoulder. It was fired from close at hand, but by whom I saw not. I have always thanked God for this, for else I had hated the man who fired, though he did but his duty to his masters. My father reeled in his saddle and was like to have fallen, but John Talboys, riding by him, held him up. The next moment my good beast falls dead with a shot, that passing my leg so close that it tore the leather of my boot, entered behind his foreleg and so passed, I take it, to his heart. Certain it is that he fell and never stirred more. The King was much concerned to see my father hurt (he had ever a tender heart for his friends, though it must be confessed that he could desert them when occasion demanded), and said to John Talboys: "Carry Colonel Dashwood to as safe a place as you can find." Thereupon they rode off at a fair

A Pikeman.

pace, my father having recovered somewhat from the first shock of his wound, I following as best I could on foot. And with this ends all that I saw of the battle of Naseby. The time was then, as near as I could reckon, about noon.

How General Cromwell fell upon the main body of the King's army, and, Sir Thomas Fairfax's reserves coming up at the same time, brake it in pieces, is known to all. The Prince came back from his idle seeking for plunder, and would have rallied them that remained, but could avail nothing. It is to be noted, indeed, that the King's men both at this and at other times lacked the steadfastness of their enemies, who would stay obstinately in their place, even when they were overborne by greater strength, and being driven back would rally again. But these things the King's men would never do; so that when they gained a victory, it was not completed, for want of a second charge, and when they suffered defeat, it was a disaster beyond all remedy. I count it, indeed, no small proof of this defect, that of our army more than a half suffered themselves to be taken prisoners, who might surely have escaped, or, it may be, restored the day, had they only had the heart to rally to each other. As for ourselves, we had in this respect great good fortune, which came about in this way. When the horsemen of the Parliament's army were riding about the field, gathering in the prisoners, Sir Thomas Fairfax comes upon us, where we were, my father lying upon the ground, and John Talboys and I sitting on either side. There was some acquaintance, or rather friendship, between the General and my father, they having met at the Court, to which my father would sometimes go, and there talking much together of military affairs, for which my Lord had had, from a boy, a very singular liking. When he saw my father, and knew who he was, he showed in his face a great concern and said, "This is a sorry sight, Master Dashwood, to behold you thus lying here. Indeed, it is the curse of this most hateful war that there is a double bitterness even in victory. They who conquer must always lament their friends that have fallen in the battle, but now we must needs lament our enemies also, who are indeed often our friends by old acquaintance and kindness. But say, can I do aught for you now?"

"Sir," said my father, "I doubt not that this bullet has sped me beyond all hope of recovery. But if, as may be, I have yet a few days to live, I would fain spend them elsewhere than in a prison. My son here is a scholar of Oxford, whom I would gladly send back to his books, now that the King's cause is lost beyond repair, as I doubt not that it is. And I would gladly have my good friend John Talboys here to take care of me till I die. Can you give me a pass that shall keep us from the prison?"

"You shall have it," said the General, "having first promised, as I doubt not you are ready to do, that you will not for the space of three years bear arms against the Parliament."

"I promise," said my father, "and that the more readily, knowing that I shall never bear arms again."

John Talboys and I also promised. Therefore the General gave to each of us a pass in these words, the name only being changed:—

"*Suffer Philip Dashwood the elder, late of the King's army, who has promised not to bear arms against the Parliament for the space of three years from this date, to pass whithersoever he will."*

This was about three of the clock in the afternoon, the battle having been then two hours ended.

CHAPTER XI.

AFTER NASEBY.

At the edge of Naseby Field, somewhere, if my memory serves me, near to the north-east corner, there was a small hollow, used in former times for digging of clay or gravel, but then overgrown with trees. It was a steep descent all round, and fenced with a paling, save in one place only, where was—or, I should rather say, had been—a road (for now the bushes almost covered it), by which the carts had been used to go down for loading of the stuff. Thither John Talboys and I carried my father, purposing to find such shelter for him for the night as the place could give, for the air was somewhat cold and nipping, as it is wont to be in these counties of the Midlands up to midsummer—yea, and past it. We had but poor provision, especially for one that was wounded, as we could not but fear, to the death. Yet with our horsemen's cloaks on some dried grass, of which we found abundance, and the saddle from my poor beast Spot for a pillow, we made a passable bed. "'Tis the very lap of luxury," said my dear father, a true soldier in every way, and in none more than in that which St. Paul will have to be a soldier's special virtue, that he can bear hardness. For food we had some eggs hard boiled and the half of a loaf of bread, and some salted pork. These were of Jack Talboys' providing. He was an old campaigner, and would as lief forget his provision of food as his musket. For myself, I had had no such forethought, and brought nothing to the common stock but the flask of sherry sack, which my good friend Master Webberley, pressed upon me when I bade him farewell. Truly, I blessed him for his forethought, for all that my father could swallow was now and then a morsel of bread sopped in the wine. It was plain to be seen that the hollow was used as a camping place by gipsies and the like, for there was a hearth where a fire had been, with great stones about it. I too would fain have lighted a fire, for the night, as I have said, was chill, and my father, for loss of blood and stiffness of his wounds, lacked warmth, but Talboys would not have it.

"There be worse things than cold," said he; "'tis not the first time that I have passed the night on the field of battle, and I liked it worse than the fighting. There be evil creatures about, I warrant you. The birds that haunt such places are no doves, but kites and carrion crows, and it would be well they should not spy us. They have a keen sight of their own, and a bit of smoke would guide them finely." So we were content to abide as we were.

I purposed to watch that night, and would have sworn that by no chance should sleep overcome me. And yet I slept, and this, if I remember right, before midnight. As long as my father was awake 'twas easy enough to resist, but when he fell into a slumber, which he did, as near as I could guess, about two hours after sunset, I soon began to nod for all my good resolutions and endeavours.

'Twas just growing light the next morning when I was awaked by voices raised in anger hard by me. Lifting myself to my feet, which for stiffness I did with no small difficulty, I saw a stranger whom John Talboys held by the collar of his coat. He was a man of a thick-set frame, somewhat under the common stature, his face burned by the sun to a very dark brown that showed somewhat strangely against his light, yellow hair, and eyes as blue as ever I saw. He had not altogether the aspect of an Englishman, and his speech, too, though ready enough, had a certain accent as of a foreigner. I liked not his look; there was somewhat greedy and cunning, ay, and cruel, too, in his face, so far as one could see it for the thick beard that he wore over his chin and lips, ay, and up to his cheek-bones.

"Nay, my good man," I heard him say to John Talboys, "I meant no harm. I am a poor pedlar, and there is my pack, which I left above, to witness for me. And see, I have not a weapon, so that I could not do any damage if I would."

"'Tis fine talking," said John Talboys, holding his coat firmly the while; "I warrant, an I searched thee, I should find a sharp knife, wherewith thou couldst shift in such warfare as thou wagest as well as with a sword or musket. Thou art a pedlar, forsooth. Doubtless, and hast other trades, too, to eke out thy profits in these hard times. Didst think to find customers in this hollow, that thou camest creeping into it? Is it thus that pedlars sell their goods, by putting their hands in men's pockets? As for thy pack, I doubt not it is there where thou sayest it is, but I reckon that thou thoughtest to carry it away hence not lighter, but heavier: a ring, or a chain, or a kerchief, or a pair of hose, or a doublet, so they were not stained by blood, would have served thy purpose well, and the better that thou payest no price for them, save a thrust with thy knife, if a man be so set against all reason that he will not part with them to an honest trader like thee for nought."

"Nay, my good friend," said the pedlar, and I noticed that his speech was the less English-like the more haste he made to get out his words, "nay, I am a Christian man, I have never harmed wounded men in my life."

"Thou a Christian man!" answered John, with great scorn and contempt; "if thou art not Judas or Barabbas by name, may I never taste spiced ale at Christmas again. I know thy sort, the eagles—God save the mark! I should say rather the carrion crows that are gathered together wheresoever the carrion is. But it was ill-luck of thine that brought thee here to-day."

Therewith John shook him as a terrier dog may shake a rat, but my father, who had been looking very steadfastly at the stranger, signified by his gesture that he should stay his hand. This done, he spake a few words in a tongue which I knew to be German, though I understood it not. The stranger grew pale, so far as his sun-burning would suffer him, and began to answer in the same language, but my father broke in upon him with, "Nay, man, speak English, for I would have no secrets from these." Thereupon the stranger said, "Do not think too ill of me, honoured sir, if I follow for a livelihood such a trade as these bad times have left me. There is but a poor market nowadays for my wares, for the war has devoured all the money in the land; and if I eke out my living by the war, what harm?"

"Nay, friend," said my father, "'tis not that war has come upon thee here, and spoilt thy trade. Thou followest the war, and thy trade is little else than a pretext and cloak for other things. Did I not see thee twenty years ago, and that many hundred miles hence, doing the same things, ay, and with the same excuse upon thy lips, that thou wast a poor trader whom the evil war time had brought to ruin? Dost remember that morning in Bohemia, and the provost-marshal's man standing with his hand on thy collar as John Talboys is standing now, ay, and another thing, that is lacking here, a gallows hard by?"

The stranger joined his hands like one that made supplication, and cast a look behind him as if he expected to see the gallows tree again.

"Nay," said my father, "I cannot harm thee an I would. Thou knowest, I doubt not, that we are three of the party that had the worst of yesterday's fight, and one of them wounded to the death. But thou wast full of promises that day thou wottest of. Hast a mind to redeem them now?"

"What can I do for you, honoured sir?"

the man answered, and I, who was looking hard at him, thought that he looked somewhat less of a knave that he did at the first.

"Tell us, then," said my father, "dost thou know of any family of charitable folk where a wounded man may bestow himself for a few days till he die? Thy pedlar's trade takes thee everywhere, and, whatever thy own ways, of which I will not judge, thou canst discern doubtless between the good and the bad."

The man stood musing awhile, then he said to himself:

"Ah! I have it. Master Ellgood is the man, an his house be not too far. This Master Ellgood," he went on, turning to my father, "is a minister that was dispossessed of his place; why I know not, for I do not understand such matters; but all the country side is full of his goodness. He asks no questions of those whom he helps; 'tis enough that they are in need. I know him and his household well, though they be but poor customers to me—a white kerchief now and then, or a bit of grey silk, or some yards of stout sad-coloured stuff, for the young madam's dress—cheap things all of them that do not pay for the carrying. But they that buy much have for the most part little to give; and Master Ellgood's folk, I doubt not, will serve thy turn better than any other in these parts. But 'tis a longish way from here, a matter of a mile and a half or more. The house stands in a wood; it had been the abode of an old curmudgeon that had never a penny to spare for pedlar or poor man; 'twas a good day for the countryside when it came with a fair estate round it to Master Ellgood. None that needed help have ever failed to have it of his hands."

"We will cast ourselves on the good man's charity," said my father. "I see in this matter the guiding of God (for 'tis not, I am assured, mere chance that sent this stranger here to-day), and we cannot do better than follow it. But how shall I make the journey?"

"That," said John Talboys, who never took his eyes from the pedlar, as if he expected him to break out into some villainy, "may easily be done; we will make a litter, and Master Philip and I will carry you."

And this we did, the pedlar, who had cunning

fingers of his own, helping. When the litter was finished, the man said, "An it please you I will be your guide, for the way is one that a stranger may readily miss; and I can take my turn of the carrying also. Only let me dispose my pack first in a safe place."

And he ran up out of the hollow more nimbly than I should have thought it possible for one of his years.

When he returned, which was in the space of a quarter of an hour or thereabouts, we went on our way. 'Twas indeed a way from which it would have been easy to go astray, so many turns it had. At last in about an hour's time, for our burden caused us to travel but slowly, we came to the house. It stood by the side of a green lane that ran through a wood, seeming to be but rarely used by horse or man. In front was a garden, passing fair with flowers, pinks and sweet-williams and a host of others; the house itself too was covered to the very eaves of the roof with roses and honeysuckle. And behind, though this I saw not at the time but only came to know afterwards, was the fairest spot that ever I saw. First there was a level space of grass, so smooth and green and well kept that our fairest lawns in Oxford could scarce compare with it. 'Twas bounded on the right hand by a low wall, grown over with ivy, and beyond this wall was a bank sloping down to as clear and fair a brook as ever babbled in man's ear. On the left hand of the green was another wall, some six feet high, with fruit trees of sundry kinds trained upon it. Beyond the green was a kitchen garden, as neatly ordered with all manner of fruits and herbs as can be conceived, and behind this again a wood sloping upwards to a height of three hundred feet and more, with the brook aforesaid leaping down through it and making, as I found afterwards, the fairest pools that can be imagined.

We rested the litter in the wood when first we came in sight of the house, and I went on alone to speak with the minister. 'Twas still early, scarce seven of the clock, if I remember, and the good man was pacing to and fro in the garden before his house, with a book in his hand, from which he read aloud as he walked.

I could hear that it was the book of Common Prayer. He was a man of taller stature than the common, but that stooped forward somewhat, and slender as a youth. I judged him then, seeing him for the first time, to have been about sixty-five years of age, but learned afterwards that I had reckoned to him ten years too many. Trouble had made him old before his time, at the least, in look, for in some matters he was, as will be seen, one of them that are ever young. There was such a sweetness in his face as passed all skill of writer's pen or painter's brush to picture; his eyes large and grey; his forehead broad, and wrinkled with many lines; his cheeks somewhat thin and tinged with a faint colour that would not have ill-beseemed a maiden's face; his lips small but full, though not over-full (over-full lips, I have noted, seem to show a passionate temper, and over-thin, a cruel); his hair, white as silver, fell almost to his shoulders. He looked, I do remember to have thought, as might an angel that had grown old. For dress he wore a cassock, tied about his middle with a woollen band of very rusty brown, and grey hose, and shoes with black buckles. On his head was a skull cap of black velvet, no less worn than the cassock.

I waited till he should see me, which, so diligently did he read his book, he did not till he paced up and down some five or six times. But when he had ended his reading of the Psalms for the morning—for it was with them that he was engaged—he looked up, saying aloud at the same time the last words of the seventy-second Psalm,* " Thou leddest Thy people like sheep by the hand of Moses and Aaron ;" and he added, "O Lord, by whom wilt Thou lead them now? for leading they sorely want!" Thereupon his eye fell on me, and I must confess that the good man started somewhat at the sight of me. Nor was this to be wondered at, for I had all the stains of battle upon me, even my face being splashed with blood. But this was but for a moment; he said, "Can I serve you, sir?" and when I had taken off my hat, " Nay, be covered." Then I set forth the whole matter to him,

* The last of the Psalms appointed for morning service on the fifteenth day of the month.

telling him of my father's estate, and of myself, and at the last showing him Sir Thomas Fairfax's paper, that he might feel the more secure in giving shelter to one that was not of the winning side. "Nay, my son," said the good man, when I showed him this last, "I need no authority to shelter the sick and wounded. For that the twenty-fifth chapter of Matthew* is authority sufficient. Yet this paper will be useful for the present distress, and save, may be, some strife and argument."

Then he called aloud, "Cicely!" whereat there came running out of the cottage a maid of some seventeen years. She was of the middle height, or somewhat more, of a fair complexion, somewhat pale, but not with the paleness of one that is troubled with sickness, her eyes of as sweet a blue as I have ever seen in a woman's face, her forehead low and somewhat broad, and her hair, that was most smoothly ordered, without any of the tricks that young maids will sometimes affect, of a singular bright chestnut colour. That I noted all these things at this first seeing of her, I cannot affirm, though

* The parable of the Judge, the sheep, and the goats.

I do believe that I did; but of this I am assured, that I deemed her at first sight to be, as indeed she was, of as sweet and virginal an aspect as ever woman had.

"Cicely," said the old man, "get ready the guest chamber, with all speed. 'Tis for a gentleman that has been sore wounded." Then, turning to me, "You had best go at once and bring your father. All things will be ready ere you come again."

So I hastened back to where I had left my father and John Talboys. And we two carried him to the cottage, and bestowed him, the old man and his daughter helping, in the guest room, which was as clean and sweet a chamber as ever I saw, though but humbly furnished. And Master Ellgood—for that was the old man's name—dressed his wound, having, as it appeared, no little knowledge of these matters.

"To find the bullet," he said, "passes my little skill, and yet it should be found. Haply we can get Master Parker from Leicester, that is the most learned surgeon in these parts. Meanwhile we will give your father such ease and comfort as we may."

I was for going without delay to Leicester, but Master Ellgood would not suffer it. "I know so much," said he, " of surgery, that I am assured that in your father's present state no man, be he the skilfullest surgeon alive, could search for and take out the bullet. Besides this, you had best not venture yourself at this present time at Leicester. I hear that the King's army took it with circumstances of no small barbarity, and I doubt whether even the Lord General's safe-conduct will avail you."

With this I was constrained to be content; but six days after Master Ellgood judged it well that the surgeon should be sent for, if perchance he might be able to come, of which, indeed, there was great doubt. Therefore, having borrowed a horse from one of the neighbours, and, indeed, it was no small favour in those days to lend a horse, and taking with me also a letter from Master Ellgood, I rode to Leicester. John Talboys had been earnest to go in my place. " Nay," said our host, "you are a soldier, and can no more hide your soldiership than you can make yourself invisible. And 'tis likely that there are some in Leicester who know your face, and haply the weight of your arm, whereas Master Philip here has been diligent at his books for many months past, and has the air of a scholar."

On the twenty-first day of June, therefore, being just one fortnight after the battle, I went to Leicester. The town was in a terrible confusion, having suffered two captures in the course of fourteen days. Many of the townsmen had fled; indeed, few were left save of the poorer sort, so that there was scarce a shop open in the place. Some were shut up, but some were still as they had been left by the soldiers that plundered them (for the town had been most cruelly sacked by the King's men), and there was scarce a window in the town that was not broken.

By great good fortune I found Master Parker, newly returned to his house, and about to sit down to his dinner. When I told him my errand, he cried out upon me: "What! ride a matter of twenty miles to see one wounded man? 'Tis manifestly impossible. Why, boy, there are two hundred wounded men within a call of this room, and some of them as curious cases as anyone could ask to see. I could fill my day three times over, and not stir a hundred yards hence."

Hearing him speak thus, I bethought me of Master Ellgood's letter, and showed it to him.

"Nay," said he, "why did you not bring this out before? There is no man whom I honour more than Thomas Ellgood, and I would ride a hundred miles to serve him. He has a pretty knowledge of physic and surgery, too, for a lay person, and perceives, too, which is a rare thing in such a case, where his knowledge ends. And now let us think how this business may be best managed. I must even make two days out of one, if the one be not long enough. We will set out about ten of the clock to-night, and so I shall be here for my day's work to-morrow. And now, sir, you must dine with me."

This I did gladly enough. Dinner ended, said Master Parker: "Divert yourself with these books. Here is Galen, and Pliny the elder, an industrious gatherer of facts, but over-credulous. Or, if you like something lighter, here are some poems by Mr. John Milton, a great friend, they tell me, of the Lord General, and here are the plays of William Shakespeare, if the saints permit me to make mention of things so profane. I would counsel you not to stir abroad, for if anyone should chance to remember you there might be some trouble."

' Nevertheless I ventured forth, being as is the wont of young men, wise in my own conceit, and save that some boys cried after me, my hair being somewhat longer than is the fashion among the puritanical folk, suffered no harm. Nay, I had some pleasant talk with an honest soldier* that I met upon the wall. He seemed, by his accent, which was such as they use in the eastern parts of England, to be but of lowly birth; but yet his talk was full of wit and fine fancy. No gentleman, were he the finest scholar in Oxford, could have spoken better. I repent me that I did not ask his name.

At ten of the clock that night we set forth, and came to Master Ellgood's house without any misadventure. Hearing that my father was

* Perhaps this common soldier was John Bunyan, who was probably in Leicester at this time.

awake, and, indeed, he rarely slept but an hour or so at one time, Master Parker would see him at once. He examined the shoulder and arm with great carefulness; and when he had made an end, my father said, "And now, sir, tell me how it is with me."

"It might have been worse," said he.

"Ay," answered my father, "if the bullet had entered some six inches more to the right it had made a shorter work with me. But whether that had been worse, who can say? save, perhaps, that a man may well have some days wherein to prepare himself. But speak out, sir; I have not faced Death so many times in the field that I should fear him in the chamber."

"'Tis not," said the surgeon, "in human skill to make a cure in this case."

"So be it," answered my father, "if such is the will of God. But tell me, sir, how long I have to live."

"Some five days I should say," the surgeon made answer.

"God reward you, sir," said my father, "for your trouble; and now, my good friends, and you, son Philip, leave me alone. When a man hears such tidings as this, though, indeed, they be nothing more than I looked for, he would fain think over them in solitude."

So we left him. About two hours after dawn the good surgeon set forth on his way back to Leicester. Looking in at my father about the same time, I saw that he was sleeping peacefully; and, indeed, he did not awake till seven of the clock, which had not happened before since his coming to the house.

CHAPTER XII.

OF MY FATHER'S END AND OTHER MATTERS.

WHEN my father awoke I asked him, "Shall I go for my mother and sister?"

He answered me: "Had I desired to see them—nay, but I do desire to see them with a great longing," and his eyes were filled with tears, a thing that I had never seen before in him; "had it been well that they should come, son Philip, I had sent you for them so soon as I was brought to this place. I knew when first that bullet struck me that it carried a billet of death, nor have I ever looked for any other end, though a man will hope even against hope, nor do I pretend to be stronger and wiser than others. But as for your mother and your sister coming hither, 'tis clearly impossible. They would need a regiment of horse to escort them safely, for the country was never so disturbed. No, my son, when I bade your mother farewell at Oxford, it was understood between us that whatever might befall me, she and our dear Dorothy should tarry at home. And, indeed, this was part of the cost that she and I counted when I took up arms for the King. God comfort her in her widowhood, and you and Dorothy render her double love and duty. And now I would settle my worldly affairs, that I may give the rest of my time to God."

After this he made a codicil to his will, to which Master Ellgood and John Talboys set their hands as witnesses. Also he bade me write down what he desired to be done with sundry possessions that he had, desiring that certain friends should have something to keep in memory of him. And he gave me many messages for kinsfolk and acquaintance, and much counsel for myself, of which the chief was that while I had the opportunity—"for how long you may have it," said he, "I know not"—I should be diligent with my books, and that in due time, if I felt any drawing thereto, I should seek for orders at the hands of a Bishop. But of these things, as being matters of private concern, I will here write no more.

The rest of his time, which was indeed but two days, the wound mortifying and so bringing him to his end sooner than any had thought, he spent in meditation and religious exercises. Master Ellgood, who was a priest, though, as will be set forth more at length hereafter, he had long been excluded from his office, was most diligent in praying and reading the Scriptures with him; and on the morning of his death, which was the festival of St. John the Baptist, delivered to him the blessed sacrament, all that were in the house communicating with him. My father's strength held out just so long that he could join, though but in a low voice, to the very end of the service. Nor did he speak again afterwards, till he came to the very last, but lay with his eyes shut, yet conscious of himself, as I knew because he pressed my hand as I sat by him. About two hours after noon it seemed to me that he had departed, for I could not see his breast move, nor feel the vein in his wrist. But it was not so, for when Cicely held a mirror to his mouth, the breath was to be seen upon it, though but very faint. In this state he lay for the space of three hours or thereabouts; but about five of the clock, there came a flush upon his cheeks, and he opened his eyes, which were as bright as ever I saw them, and looked at me, and said in a clear voice, smiling the while: "I have seen her, and it is well." And having said this he passed away. And here I should say that at this very hour my mother sitting in her chamber, having just come back from evensong in St. Peter's Church, saw my father, as plain as ever she had seen him in life, standing by the window; and that he smiled upon her very sweetly and pleasantly. "I seemed to know," she said afterwards, "that it was not he in the flesh, for I did not make to go to him or speak to him; but yet I was in no wise afraid, but sat looking at him with such love and gladness in my heart as I had never felt before. And in a short space of time, for it seemed to me, but 'twas, as afterwards I found from comparing of time, about half of an hour, he vanished out of my sight."

My father was buried in the churchyard of Naseby, Master Ellgood saying over him the service provided in the Prayer Book. The minister of Naseby, a good man, but somewhat timid withal, had not dared to use it, but our host had no such fear. "None," said he, "will hinder me or call me to account." And so it was, I may note, that, having the whole by heart from beginning to end, he used no book. Maybe, had he had a book in his hand, some that were present might have made objection; but when he said it as if extempore, not only did none murmur, but all seemed edified. 'Tis a strange thing, and yet of a piece with many other things in life, that a man may say unharmed, yea, and commended, that which to read would put him in peril of liberty or life.

I, coming back from the burying, was wetted through by a great storm of rain, and, neglecting to change my clothes, was the next day taken with a great cold and fever, other things, I doubt not, as care and trouble of mind, making the sickness worse. And, indeed, 'twas so sore (this they told me after, but at the time I knew nothing, but only raved of fighting and of disputing in the school at Oxford), that for some days I was like to follow my father. So I lay betwixt life and death till it was about the middle of the month of July; and then partly through Master Ellgood's skill in physic (especially in the use of simples of which he had a considerable knowledge), and more through the good nursing of Mistress Cicely and of John Talboys, I began to mend.

One morning when the danger was past, says John Talboys to me, "'Tis time, sir, that I thought of departing hence. You need me no more, and I must shift for myself. My soldiering is over for three years to come; but I reckon that a stout pair of hands will not lack employment. I can ply a sickle and drive a furrow as well as most men; and there are those in Oxfordshire who know it and will give me good wages."

So I gave him two gold pieces (having had ten given me by my father). He was loath to take them, but I pressed them on him, as being my father's gift to him, as indeed they were. Also I wrote a letter of many sheets to my mother, which I gave into his keeping, he promising to deliver it into her hands with all possible speed. So he departed; nor have I ever seen him again, but I hear that he prospers;

keeping an inn at Cassington, in the county of Berks, and having also a farm. He is as brave and honest a fellow as ever bestrode a horse.

After I began to mend I saw no more of Mistress Cicely, though I could hear her singing about the house, for she had a very sweet and tunable voice. There waited on me a very decent widow woman from the village, that was reckoned a notable nurse in these parts; such doubtless she was, for I never lacked anything, but had all things served at the due time. But she had a heavy hand, and a croaking voice, and was of a singular doleful temper. She would sit by the hour and talk to me of those whom she had nursed in times past, and if she mentioned one that had died she would say like enough, "He very greatly favoured you, sir," or "He had the same complexion as you, and I have noted that it often goes with a consumption," or "He was of very tall stature, and your tall men fail very suddenly." I was myself tall. As for her readiness to believe all kinds of marvels, 'twas such as I never saw surpassed. There was scarce a house in the country but she knew of some ghost that walked in it, and if there was no ghost of a man, then there was one of a dog or a cat; and as for witches, there was not a village but had two or three. And when I doubted, she had circumstances at hand to prove what she said. "Did not Thomas Clark at Erpington Mill speak roughly to Alice Viner, the Erpington witch, for picking wood in his coppice, and Alice cursed him, and said that he should never die in his bed, and the miller, coming home from market the very next Tuesday, fell from his horse and was killed?" "But was the miller in liquor, think you?" I said. "Yes," said she, "and had come home in liquor every market day for thirty years and more, and had come to no harm till he fell out with Alice." That witches may be, I do not doubt, for does not Scripture say, "Thou shalt not suffer a witch to live;" but that many poor women have an ill-name for witchcraft, ay, and worse than an ill-name, that have no worse faults than a shrewish temper and a bitter tongue, I do not doubt. With such doleful tales did Margery Marriott—for that was the good woman's name—entertain me; and though Master Ellgood would come and sit with me,

I was right glad, when the fever having left me and, in a great measure, the weakness also that followed it, I was quit of her company.

It was about the end of July when I left my chamber; there then followed so delightful a time as had never before come to me in my whole life. First, the skies smiled upon me, for the summer having been hitherto somewhat wet and stormy, there now began a season of the most serene weather that can be imagined; and next, the place was most sweet and pleasant, a very home of peace, and Master Ellgood showed me such courtesy and kindness as could not be surpassed; and lastly, to use the figure which the rhetoricians call a climax, I had sometimes at least, though not as often as I would, the companionship of Mistress Cicely. Of her face and aspect I have written before; and these were such, indeed, as would strike all beholders; but of the inner beauty and fairness of her soul, I have said nothing, nor, indeed, can now say enough. She ordered her father's household with such nice care as not the most experienced matron could have excelled, and yet had barely ended her seventeenth year; nay, but for the help of a little maid and a lad that hewed the wood and fetched the water, she did all the service of the house; yet, for all this, I never saw her with so much as a pin awry, nor any flush upon her cheeks, though she might be newly come from cooking the dinner. And for all these cares, yet time never failed her to minister to the sick when any needed her help; no, nor to nourish her own mind with the reading of wholesome authors. She was not ignorant of Latin, which her father had taught her in company with her brother, but to this, since he went to the war, she had paid but little heed; but with our English writers she had such acquaintance as made me, being indeed somewhat rude in these matters, wholly ashamed. 'Twas of her that I learnt to read the *Canterbury Pilgrims* of Geoffrey Chaucer, and the poems of Lord Surrey, and the incomparable Sir Philip Sidney's romance of *Arcadia*. Of William Shakespeare his plays I knew already somewhat, but with her and her father much increased my knowledge, for of an evening we would read one or another, dividing the characters among ourselves. But I must confess that it was not her notable housekeeping, nor her charitable disposition, nor her learning in authors ancient and modern, that I chiefly admired in her; no, nor her beauty only, that I may be but just to myself; but herself, that was a compound, most sweetly mixed of all; for gracious ways, and a delicate courtesy, and a most modest discretion of voice and look set off and displayed, if I may so speak of that which did always rather seek to hide itself, the singular virtues of her mind and body. I do believe what divines teach of the corruption of human nature, yet I must confess that I have seen women, of whom Cicely Ellgood was one, my mother another, and my sister Dorothy a third, in whom I never discovered that which could rightly be called corrupt. Faults they had, I doubt not, though in Cicely and my mother I never perceived any such (for Dorothy had a quick temper, but only in too hot anger against wrong-doing); but that they sinned—if I must need receive it, I receive it of faith, not of understanding.

I do not know whether Master Ellgood perceived how I was affected towards his daughter, for that I was greatly enamoured of her scarcely needs telling; but on the seventh day, or thereabouts, after my first descending from my chamber, he called me to his private parlour, saying that he desired to have some talk with me.

"Master Dashwood," he said; "'tis well that host and guest, if their chance acquaintance has any likelihood to become more durable, should know something of each other. Hear, therefore, my story; it may be that, having heard it, you may choose that we should part. I was—nay, I do protest that I still am—a priest of the Church of England; but I have been for these many years deprived of my office; and the cause was this, which you shall now hear. May be you have not heard of the *Book of Sports*. It made trouble enough in its days, but like enough has now been forgotten for stress of graver matters.

It had this for its title: *Concerning Lawful Sports to be used on Sundays after Divine Service.* In it was commanded that dancing and archery, and May games, and Whitsun ales, and Church feasts, should be held lawful; but bull-baiting and bear-baiting and interludes forbidden. At its first publishing it made but little stir; this was some thirty years since, in the days of King James I. But when Dr. Laud, that was then Archbishop of Canterbury, put it forth again some twelve years since, and strictly commanded all the Bishops of his province that they should enforce it on all ministers, no little trouble arose. Against Dr. Laud I would say nothing, but he was one that suffered not his words to fall to the ground. There went out, therefore, a strict commandment that every minister should read the book on the eighteenth of October following—being St. Luke's day—publicly in the church, after morning prayer. Some of the bishops took little heed of the matter; but my Lord of Norwich, in whose diocese I held a cure, was exceeding hot about it. To be brief, I read it not. Now I hold not with them who mislike these games altogether. If the Jews danced and shot with the bow, why not Christian men? And as for the Whitsun ales and the Church feasts and the like, that they work mischief I deny not; but 'tis chiefly because honest and sober folk keep too much aloof from them, and leave them to the looser sort. Nor am I altogether resolved in mind whether such things be unlawful on the Sunday. To forbid them savours of Sabbath worship; yet to permit them does not tend to edifying. May be you will ask why then did I not read the book, as was enjoined upon me? Because I held that the civil power was intruding into things with which it had no concern, the which intrusion every true minister of God must resist to the loss of all things, and, if need be, even to the death. Howbeit I will not weary you with my reasons, which, indeed, that I may be altogether honest, I found not many to comprehend. To the one party I seemed a rebel, because I obeyed not my ordinary, and to the other a profane person, because I condemned not the sports. Let my reasons, therefore, be. 'Tis enough for my present purpose to say that I could not in my conscience obey. Well, the Archbishop being advised by my Lord of Norwich, sends for me to Lambeth. As soon as I came into his library, where he sat with a chaplain on either hand, he burst out on me: 'Well, sir, I hear that you read not the book on the day appointed. Is it so?' 'Suffer me, your Grace——' I said; but before I could end my sentence he cried out, 'Answer me "yea" or "nay."' 'I read it not,' said I, being myself also, it must be confessed, a little touched by his heat. 'Then,' he cried, in a loud voice, 'I suspend you for ever from your office and benefice till you shall read it.' Thereat I saw one of the chaplains whisper into his ear. Hereupon he moderated somewhat his voice, and said, 'Have you any defence?' I had written down my reasons, and now began to read them. They were, as I have said already, that the book was a civil declaration, such as could not lawfully be enforced by any court ecclesiastical. But when I had read barely a page he brake in upon me: 'Hold! 'tis enough; I will hear no more. Whosoever shall make such a defence, it shall be burned before his face, and he laid by the heels in prison. Hear now; I admonish you hereby, personally and judicially, that you read this Declaration within three weeks, under pain of being suspended *ab officio et beneficio*.' As I turned to go I saw that the chaplain whispered in his ear again. Then the Archbishop said, 'Tarry a moment, Master Ellgood, and sit down'—for hitherto I had been standing—'I would have a word with you.' And this he said in a voice more gentle by far than he had before used. Afterwards I heard that the chaplain had whispered to him about a little book that I had written of St. Cyprian and the Bishop of Rome, in which matter the Archbishop was much concerned. 'Have you studied the Fathers, Master Ellgood?' And when I confessed that I had some knowledge of them, he held me in talk about sundry matters which were then much talked of, of which the chief was the supremacy of the Bishop of Rome. This converse held us till noon, when the Archbishop would have me dine with him, and, dinner ended, we played at bowls, the day being fine, though it was already November; and I throwing my bowls well— for I have always loved the game—his Grace said, ''Tis not now the first time that you have thrown a bowl, Master Ellgood, so that you mislike not all sport.' This he spake right pleasantly, and when I went away he gave me his blessing, and said, 'I doubt not, Master Ellgood, but that we shall agree;' and so parted from me in all friendship. Of a truth, I would fain have done his pleasure, if only conscience had suffered me; but I must needs wrap me in my virtue, if I may somewhat misquote Horace; nor could I consent that the sun of his Grace's favour should cause me to cast off that which the blast of his wrath had not rent from me. I stood, therefore, by my denial, and so was first excommunicated, and afterwards, still persisting, deprived of my benefice. Ah, my son! 'twas a hard time with me and mine; nor has it always been an easy thing with me to be in charity with all men. They drave me forth from my house in February, when the snow was lying deep upon the ground; and for two days we had no shelter for our heads but a barn. The Bishop's people stripped me of all that I had, but 'twas not of my lord's knowledge, and I had not so much as a piece of silver in my pocket, nor did any man dare to take me into his house, though some brought me food by stealth. My wife was stricken of so deadly a chill that she fell into a wasting sickness and died some three months after. She had taken some of her underclothing to keep our children the warmer; but this I knew not till after. Perchance it was better that I knew not; it had been a hard thing to choose between mother and children. But why do I weary you with my troubles? Suffice it to say that for two years I could scarce keep body and soul together. A trifle I earned translating for the booksellers, and the dedication of two little treatises that I wrote fetched me a few guineas; but I had received better wages by following the plough, had but my hands been hard enough. Some of my brethren in the ministry also helped, especially Dr. Thomas Fuller, that was vicar of Broadwinsor, and some money I had from the Archbishop himself, but this I knew not till after his death. God forgive me for thinking too hardly of him! At the end of the two years, a certain kinsman that, living, had never favoured me, dying without a will, I inherited this house, with some two hundred acres of land, part of which I have farmed as best I could, and part have let. Perchance you would ask why, they that persecuted me having fallen from power, I have had no favour from them that succeeded to their place? The cause is soon said. I am no Puritan; I hold neither with Presbyterian nor with Independent, but think that bishops are the true rulers of the Church, though I myself have had scant favour from them. The Covenant I cannot subscribe, nor can I satisfy the Committees that the Parliament has appointed for the examining of the clergy. An I could, I would not intrude myself into a benefice from which some godly man has been driven out because he was faithful to his King. But enough of myself. If you can bear with one who can neither run with the hare nor hunt with the hounds, well; I shall rejoice from my heart; but if not, we can at the least part in Christian charity."

I should have found it hard to part with sweet Cicely's father had he been Hugh Peters himself, who was the loudest and fiercest of all the Parliament preachers. But who could refuse the hand of fellowship to such an one as

William Ellgood? He was one of those whose consciences are too fine set for this world. Whoever was uppermost, there would be ever some thing at which he would have some scruple. He had fared just as ill, nay worse, had he lived a hundred years before. Then he had been condemned under the Six Articles, and fallen under the displeasure of the counsellors of King Edward, and been in danger of the fire at Smithfield, and been deprived of his benefice under Queen Elizabeth. Verily he was no vicar of Bray that would be vicar still whoever should rule the roast. The more I knew him the more I loved him, yet I could but see that were all men such as he, life itself would be a thing impossible. Pure he was, and single-minded and steadfast, but could see but one thing at a time; and everything, be it ever so small, was an article of faith to him, for which he had gone cheerfully to the death; and I soon learnt to see so much, not only in his talk, in which he afterwards was quite free with me, but in his face, which, for all its angelical sweetness, had a certain set look which I have noted in the fiercest sectaries. But William Ellgood was one that had for others a charity without bounds, and was stern only upon himself.

Two or three days after Master Ellgood opened to me a trouble that he had about his son. "He is a good lad," he said to me, "my son John, but he does not see eye to eye with me in matters of Church and State. There is work enough for them who stand aside from both parties in these days, and this I would have had him do, but he was not content, but must needs take service with the Parliament. He was with my Lord Essex's army, and is promoted, I believe, to be a captain; but the whole matter is a sore trouble to me."

"Well, Master Ellgood," said I, "I had been better pleased had he stood for the King; but that one who hath the strength to strike a blow should stand aside and not deal it for one side or the other, is not to be looked for."

"Say you so?" said he; "there are but few that have one mind with me in this matter. I must e'en be content to be alone."

I sojourned six weeks with Master Ellgood and then departed, though, as need scarce be said, very loath to go, but I heard that his son John, the war being now well nigh at an end, was like to return home, and I could not reconcile it to myself to see him, when he had lately borne arms against the King. I spake no word to Mistress Cicely before I went, for who was I—a poor scholar that had followed the losing side—to entangle her with promises? But there are vows that pass without words. Such an one I made in my own heart. As for her, I knew nothing certain, and lovers will find their hopes in slight tokens; yet such a hope I found; and it sent me away with a lighter heart than I had ever looked to have again.

CHAPTER XIII.

OF MY COMING BACK TO OXFORD.

COMING back to Oxford about the beginning of the month September, I found all things in a very disheartened condition. For, indeed, little now remained to the King. The strong city of Bristol the Prince Rupert had surrendered to the Lord General, having but a few days before affirmed in a letter to the King that he could hold the place for four months unless he should be constrained otherwise by mutiny in the garrison. The King, indeed, was ill-served by this same Prince, of whom it may be said that he was over bold where he needed to be cautious, and that where boldness was most required he showed no small lack of constancy. About the same time also there came news of the defeat of my Lord Montrose, at Philiphaugh. From him the King had hoped great things; and, indeed he had had for a time singular great success; but his army was such that success was no less fatal to it than defeat, the savage people from the Highlands, who were its mainstay, retiring, after their custom, to the mountains, where they dwelt, when they had gathered a sufficiency of plunder. As for the King himself, he was then at Newark, to which place he had fled, with but a small following, from Chester, where, seeking to relieve the city from siege, he had been defeated with great loss. But about the beginning of November (for it was, I remember about the day of our *Gaudeamus*—that is to say, the first day of November) he came back to Oxford, and there tarried for the rest of the winter.

And now it was needful to prepare all things for the worst. First, then, because it could not be hoped but that the city of Oxford would be soon besieged (a thing which, though many times threatened, had never yet been done), it seemed good to make perfect the fortifications. There came forth, therefore, a proclamation from his Majesty's Privy Council that all the inhabitants of Oxford, being above the age of sixteen, should upon four several days, named therein, work upon the fortifications behind Christ Church (at which place their defect was greatest). And it was ordered that if any person from age, or infirmity, or other occupation, should fail so to work, he should either find one suitable person to labour in his stead, or should pay a contribution of one shilling for the day; and for each servant the householder employing him was to pay the sum of sixpence. Having but few shillings in my purse, and being curious withal to see the matter, which was indeed a new thing in England, I elected to work rather than to pay. And, indeed it was a strange sight to see the multitude gathered together. Some came for very zeal, as if they could not be content but they must show how zealous they were for the King, and some for meanness or poverty came rather to labour with their own hands than to pay. So far as I could see there was but little work done, and this from lack of skill in part, and in part from want of heart. I verily believe that a hundred stout fellows paid, not by the hours of their working, but by the work that they should do, had

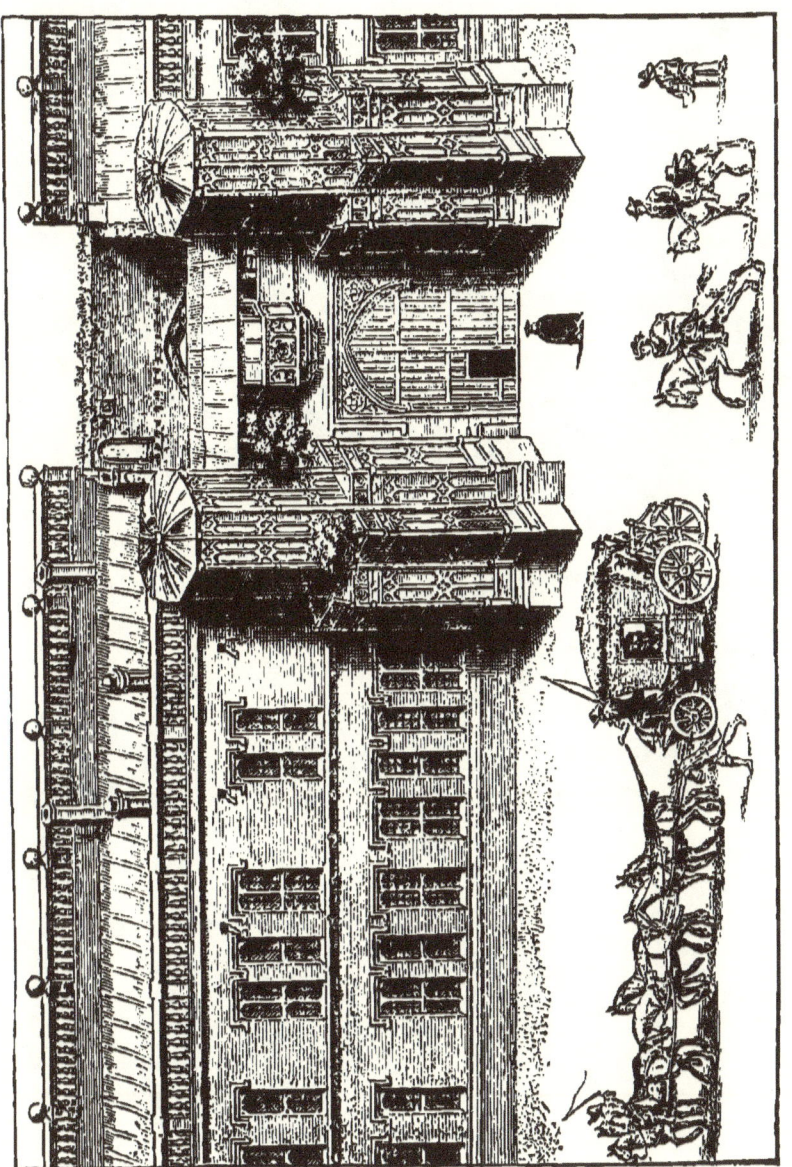

The Gateway of Christ Church, Oxford.

accomplished much more than the mixed multitude gathered together that day.

The fortifications, however, be they as strong as they might, could defend the city but for a short time only, and, indeed, had their chief use in this, that the garrison and inhabitants, being safe from sudden assault, might through them obtain for themselves better terms of surrender. It was necessary, therefore, to provide, so far as might be possible, against the time when the city should be surrendered into the hands of our enemies. Of this provision one chief matter was the hiding away of such things as were apt to suffer damage from their hatred or ignorance. Now there had come from time to time grievous reports of the cruel damage done by the soldiers of the Parliament in various cathedrals and churches throughout the realm wherever they had fallen into their power. Especially had they shown themselves zealous against what in their fanatic language they were wont to call idolatry, not only breaking down statues that they espied on walls or on tombs, but also figures, whether of Christ or of holy men that were painted on windows. And it was known that they were especially zealous against such figures or images when they savoured of Popery, as ran the phrase which was greatly in favour in these times. Such things then it seemed expedient to hide. Therefore at Christ Church, in the Cathedral, the Dean, than whom there was no one more stiff for the King, had a certain window, which is especially prized in that Society, put away in a safe place, and another set up in its place. On this window was represented Dr. Robert King, last Abbot of Oseney and first Bishop of Oxford, in his bishop's robes, having a mitre on his head and holding a crosier in his right hand. 'Twas most handsomely painted with colours, so fine and so harmoniously blended as no man in these days seems to have the wit to do. I hope that it may remain hidden so long as these present hardships may endure, and be found when they shall have passed away, as I do not doubt that they will. At Magdalen College, also, the painted glass of the great eastern window in the chapel was taken out of its place, and put away in like manner, for the safe restoration of which I here set down the same hope.

The last Abbot of Oseney.

On the fourteenth day of March in the year following (that is to say, the year 1646) an army of Sir Ralph Hopton, that still held out for the King in Cornwall (and 'twas in the West that his Majesty's cause was ever the strongest, whereas it was weakest in the East) surrendered itself, being reduced to such straits as left no hope of escape, much less of victory. This was heard in Oxford, by a messenger from the general of the enemy, who was so courteous as to give us the news, not the less readily perhaps, that it was not like to be welcome. On the very same day, that is the twenty-second day of March (for the matter in Cornwall, having befallen on the fourteenth, had taken so long to travel to us) came tidings of a great misfortune that had befallen his Majesty nearer at hand. For Sir Jacob Astley, coming from Worcester to Oxford with about three thousand men, mostly horse, that he had gathered, was fallen upon by one Colonel Morgan at Stow-on-the-Wold, and routed, being himself taken prisoner. This we heard from one of Sir Jacob's own riders, who escaped, or, I should rather suppose, was suffered to escape, that he might bring the ill news to the King. And, indeed, 'twas the very last stroke that overset the tottering edifice of his fortunes, as was sufficiently evident from what the good knight, being taken to the aforesaid Colonel Morgan, is reported to have said: "Now you have done your work, and may go to play, unless you choose to fall out among yourselves." Of this same valiant soldier is told another thing which seems to me well worthy to be here set down, that at the battle of Edgehill, before he charged, he made this prayer: "O Lord! Thou knowest how busy I must be this day. If I forget Thee, do not Thou forget me." And having said so much, he rose from his knees, and cried with a cheerful voice, "March on, boys."

And now, a siege being imminent, the King departed from Oxford. Of his going but very few knew beforehand, but I heard afterwards from one that was present that he went at midnight on the twenty-seventh day of April, being disguised as a servant, even to having his hair cut in Puritan fashion, and riding with a portmanteau behind him. He had but two companions, Dr. Hudson, that was a parson, but not less a soldier, and a certain Master Ashburnham, whose servant he feigned himself to be. And if few knew of his purpose of going, the place whither he should go he knew not himself. At the first he rode towards London, to which, indeed, he approached so near that he came as far as Harrow-on-the-Hill being minded, it was said, to enter the City and throw himself on the mercy of the Parliament. But, departing from this purpose, if, indeed, he ever entertained it, he rode northward to Newark, where the Scots' army lay, hoping that they might protect him, of which hope he was, indeed, grievously disappointed, the Scots giving him up to his enemies. 'Twas said that they sold him; and it is certain that at the time of his being surrendered, it was agreed that the Scots should have four hundred thousand pounds, being, as they said, arrears of their wages, paid to them. Yet, as they came into England to make war, together with the Parliament, against the King, this charge, methinks, is too harsh, for being by profession enemies, why should they behave to him as friends? Nevertheless it had been more seemly if no mention had been made at the time of the wages.

And now at Oxford the end came nearer and nearer. We made a dam at St. Clement's Bridge (which is by Magdalen College), and so laid the country that is to the south side of the city under water. But elsewhere the lines of the enemy were drawn all about us. This was the beginning of May. Of fighting there was but little; on this, being, as I conceived, bound by my oath, I did not so much as look. But I could not choose but hear the cannonading which went forward with but little rest. Our men would fire, it was said, so many as two hundred shots in the day, doing, however, but small damage, so that it seemed as if they had it in their mind to spend their powder rather than to do execution. And I take it that they suffered more damage than they gave, the enemy having more marks, and these also more manifest, at which to make his aim. About the ending of the month of May comes an order from the King that the city should be surrendered.

Meanwhile I, as I have said, turned away

not only my hands, but also, as far as it was possible, my eyes and my thoughts from war, conceiving that I should so acknowledge the great kindness of my Lord Fairfax. Here, therefore, I may not unfittingly set down somewhat about the thing with which I now concerned myself. Before my going to join company with my father before the battle at Naseby, being about to finish my second year of residing, I performed my first exercises, that is to say, I answered, as the Academical phrase has it, *in parviso*, and so became, to use again the somewhat barbarous dialect, *sophista generalis*, the visible signs and tokens of which honour was the putting into my hands of a book of Aristotle, and round my neck, by one of the bedels, when I had duly finished my answering, of a little hood of some common black stuff, which same hood, as might be concluded from its look, had done the like service for many before me.

As I am speaking of this matter I may anticipate the time somewhat in this place, and relate how I afterwards answered for my degree, which by great fortune I was able to do before that I was constrained to leave Oxford. The questions on which I disputed were in part ethical, and in part philosophical. And here, for the edifying of my readers, I will set them forth, being two of each sort. First, then, came the philosophical.

1. *Whether there can be administered by the art of the physician an universal remedy?*

2. *Whether the moon can be inhabited? And whether, it being granted that it has inhabitants, these have a popular or a despotic constitution?*

After these came the ethical questions, in which were included political.

1. *Whether the die be a lawful means of acquiring property?*

2. *Whether a multitude of scholars be profitable to a commonwealth?*

But this was not done till after the time of which I have been now speaking, when I was near upon completing my fourth academical year.

CHAPTER XIV.

OF BODLEY'S LIBRARY.

'TIS no small pleasure for me, and will be doubtless for any that shall hereafter read what I have here written, to turn from wars and fighting, of which I must perforce say much, to the quiet and delectable realm of learning. And, though I would not be thought wilfully to praise myself, I may say so much that, amidst all the distractions of the time, which were indeed many and great, this realm I did never wholly leave or desert, though compelled often to be absent therefrom.

Having already spoken of these matters, I would now say somewhat of that place which is, as it were, the capital of this kingdom to such as are subjects thereof, within the limits of the

University of Oxford—I speak of Bodley's Library. This I do the more willingly because I know not how long it may abide unharmed in its present estate. For who knows not what shameful things were done, when, one hundred years ago, or thereabouts, the visitors of King Edward, sixth of the name, purged, as they did call it, the libraries of this place, and among them that noble collection of manuscripts and books which Humphrey, Duke of Gloucester, and Thomas Kempe, some time Bishop of London, with other benefactors, did bestow upon the University of Oxford. Their commission was to do away with all that savoured of Popish superstition. If, therefore, they spied in any volume any illumination or picture, or even rubrical letter, such as are wont to be used for the ornamentation of mass-books and the like, that they incontinently destroyed without further examination, for such examination they had not the will, or, it may be, the ability to make. Such, indeed, was their ignorance, if one may believe the tradition that is yet current in Oxford concerning this matter, that such books wherein appeared angles or mathematical diagrams were thought sufficient to be destroyed, because accounted Popish, or diabolical, for, indeed, they stood in no less dread of witchcraft than of the Pope. Nay, their folly had almost led them into the grossest impiety, for among the books brought out to be destroyed were, 'tis said, many copies of the New Testament in Greek, which, the character being strange to them that handled them, were condemned as mischievous, and had perished together with the rest, but that one wiser than his fellows kept them from their fate. Certain it is that damage beyond all counting was done in this way, the rage of these ignorant men being especially directed against the works of Peter Lombard, and Thomas Aquinas, and Duns Scotus, and others, who are commonly called the Schoolmen. These were carried on biers by rude young men of the city to the market-place, and there, being piled in a great heap, burned with fire. Others, against which they had no special hate, were sold, and at such mean rates that one knows not whether to be more angry or ashamed at their silliness. For what says John Bale on this matter, who, as all know, was no lover of monks and monkery, but rather hated all that savoured of Papistry with a perfect hatred. He says that many reserved these books to scour their candlesticks and to rub their boots; that others they sold to grocers and soap-sellers, and some they sent over to the bookbinders, whole shipsful at a time, to the wonderment of foreign nations. And again, descending to particulars, he writes: "I know a merchant man, which shall at this time be nameless, that bought the contents of two noble libraries for forty shillings price: a shame it is to be spoken. This stuff hath he occupied in the stead of grey paper by the space of more than these ten years, and yet he hath store enough for as many years to come." All that bought them made not such an ill use of their purchase. God be thanked therefore! Thus a certain Dutchman, by trade a stationer, living in St. Mary's Parish, bought some, which, being handed down by him to his son, were in the end given to the Library when Sir Thomas Bodley did restore it.

So much for the past, which I have here written down because I hold it to be not impossible that the like may be done again. For the present, indeed, this fate has been warded off, for when, as I shall hereafter relate, this City of Oxford was delivered up to the Parliament, the Lord-General did straightway set a guard to keep the Library from all harm; and this he did, being a lover of learning, and well knowing that there were in the army many persons who, having a zeal without knowledge, would have utterly destroyed it. And, indeed, I know, not whether these may not yet so prevail as to get the chief regimen of things into their own hand, for, as all history teaches us, the course of things in all such revolutions as this that hath lately overthrown the constitution of this country is this: first, the moderate and discreet have power; next, these either yield to the more violent and extreme or are themselves carried away by their own headway; and last, when the folly and wickedness of this excess has become altogether unendurable, the old order is again set up. Meanwhile, being desirous above all things to follow the truth, and to be just to all men, I must acknowledge that so far more damage was done to the Library by the King's friends while they held the city than has since been done by his enemies, many books having been embezzled, the chains by which the more precious are bound to their places being cut off, and other injuries done. But to come back to my subject.

Sir Thomas Bodley's Library, then, is a spacious building, of which the main chamber lies east and west, having ten windows on either side, and furnished in most goodly sort with shelves and other needful appurtenances. The chief glory of this chamber is the roof, divided into squares, on each of which are painted the arms of the University, being the open Bible with the seven seals, of which St. John speaks in the Revelation (but others take it of the seven liberal arts), and the words, "DOMINUS ILLUMINATIO MEA."* On the bosses that are between each compartment are painted the arms of Sir Thomas Bodley himself. At the east end of this chamber is the bust of the pious founder, Sir Thomas

* "The Lord is my Light."

The Bodleian Library, Oxford.

Bodley, who has been dead at this present time of writing (1651) eight-and-thirty years. Of this bust King James I., visiting the Library three years after his coming to the throne, said, having read the well-merited praises that have been inscribed there, "Verily, his name should be *Godley* rather than Bodley." The wit of this saying is indeed but indifferent, but it has what all wit does not possess, that is to say, truth. To this chamber has been added at the eastern end what may be called a picture gallery, also furnished with bookshelves, which occupies the whole of the upper story of the quadrangle.

So much of the building, but of the precious things which it contains I cannot profess to speak. Of printed books there must be near upon thirty thousand, a number which it staggers the mind only to conceive; but as for reading them, not the life-time of Methuselah himself would suffice.* Of manuscripts also there is a great store, some of them being most uncommonly rare and precious, as, for

* What would Philip Dashwood have said of the *three hundred thousand volumes* of which the Library now consists?—A.C.

example, to mention one only out of many, is a manuscript of the Gospels, sent by St. Gregory to St. Augustine, his missionary to this realm of England, a treasure long preserved in St. Augustine's Abbey in the City of Canterbury, and given to this Library some fifty years since by Sir Robert Cotton. In this temple of the Muses, then, to speak the language of Paganism, I was accustomed to spend many hours; at the first, while I was as yet an undergraduate, by favour and recommendation of Master Webberley, of whom I have before spoken, and afterwards, having been admitted to the degree of Bachelor, of my own right. 'Tis rich in books of that classical learning which I have always, so far as it has been possible for me, especially followed, and most conveniently ordered for students, to whom indeed it is specially commended by the courtesy of its officers.* 'Twas indeed but little visited by readers in my time, the Muses having been driven out both there and elsewhere by the tumult of arms. Yet there were some faithful students who seemed not to care one jot who

*Still a tradition of the Library.—A.C.

ruled the realm so that they were not disturbed in this their peculiar province; as for me, my young blood permitted me not to reach so serene a height, but I never suffered myself to be wholly distracted from study, as were many of my fellows, by the excitements of war. I have myself seen more than once the King come into the Library, desiring to see some book that was therein. This he did because Bodley's statutes forbid the lending out of any book or manuscript, be the borrower who he may. But I remember that in the year 1645, while I was reading in the great chamber (I bear in mind that it was winter time and passing cold), there came an order to Master Rous, then and now Bodley's Librarian, in these words: " Deliver unto the bearer hereof, for the present use of his Majesty, a book intituled *Histoire Universelle du Sieur d'Aubigné*, and this shall be your warrant." To this Dr. Samuel Fell, Dean of Christ Church and then Vice-Chancellor, had subscribed, " His Majesty's use is in command to us." But Master Rous would have none of it, having sworn to observe the statutes of the Library, which statutes forbid all lending of the books without any respect of persons. Therefore he goes to the King and shows him the statutes, which being read, the King would not have the book nor permit it to be taken out of the Library, saying that it was fit that the will and statutes of the pious founder should be religiously observed. Would that he had been like-minded in all things! So much I may say without damage to my fidelity. It had been happier so for him and for this realm of England.

And thus I am reminded of a strange thing that I heard from the lips of Master Verneuil, who was in those days Deputy-Librarian. The King, coming into the Library on a certain day, was shown a curious copy of the poet Virgil. Then the Lord Falkland that was with him (the same that was slain at the second battle of Newbury, to the great loss of this realm and sorrow of all the better sort on either side) would have his Majesty make trial of his fortune by the *Sortes Virgilianæ*. This is a kind of augury which has been very much used for some ages past, the manner of it being thus: The person that will consult the oracle, if I may so speak, taking a penknife or bodkin in his hand, thrusts it, turning his head away at the same time, into the volume of Virgil. This done, he opens the book and takes the place to which the instrument may point as the answer that Fate intends for him. On this occasion, therefore, the King lighted upon this period, being part of the imprecation which Queen Dido invokes on Æneas that has deserted her. It was Englished thus by Master Thomas Phaer, about one hundred years since.

"Yet let him vexed be with arms and wars of peoples wild,
And hunted out from place to place, an outlaw still exiled.
And let him beg for help, and from his child dissevered be,
And death and slaughter vile of all his kindred let him see,
And when to laws of wicked peace he doth himself behight,
Yet let him never reign, nor in this life to have delight,
But die before his day, and rot on ground without a grave."

The King being in no small degree discomposed at this accident, the Lord Falkland would himself make trial of the book, hoping to fall on some passage that should have no relation to his case, that so the King's thoughts might be in a measure diverted from the impression that had been made upon them. But, lo! it fell out that the place he stumbled upon was yet more suited to his destiny than that other had been to the King. 'Twas in the eleventh book of the Æneid where the old King Evander speaks of the death of Pallas his son. This was Englished by Master Thomas Twynam, who finished the work of Master Phaer aforesaid.

"Didst not, O Pallas, thou to me, thy sire, this promise make:
That charily thou wouldst thyself to cruel war betake?
I knew right well the novel pride, and glory first in fight,
And pleasant honour won in arms how much prevail it might.
O hard beginnings to a lad and woeful martial train!"

So much then for the Library of Sir Thomas Bodley.

CHAPTER XV

OF THE VISITORS AT OXFORD

OF the surrendering the city there is no need for me to write. Let it suffice to say that, after parleys held for certain days, the articles of agreement were signed on the twenty-third day of June, and on the day following the city was delivered over to Sir Thomas Fairfax. I remember it by this token, that it was the feast of St. John the Baptist, and that Master Blagrove, of whom more hereafter, preached before the University on that day in the Chapel of St. John's College, as the custom is. The garrison went forth with their flags flying, and all the honours of war, and many others went with them.

Of these, some had nought to do with the University, having been brought to Oxford by the war, and now leaving it in due course when they thought they might serve the King elsewhere (though, indeed, his cause was now past help, save from the hand of God, and this was for the time present stayed). Others left place and preferment, or the prospect of such, in their several colleges, either because from the long use of arms to which they had been accustomed, by the siege the pursuits of peace had become flat and unprofitable, or because they were so well known as enemies to the cause of the Parliament that they did not venture to stay behind; or, finally, as was the case with not a few, as conceiving that their duty to the King was best done elsewhere than in Oxford. As for myself, though not yielding to any in loyalty to his sacred Majesty, I remained where I was. To this I conceived myself bound, not only by promise to the Lord General Fairfax, but also by my father's instructions, who had laid it upon me as a command that I should follow my studies so long as it should be possible. Also I had a duty to my mother and sister which I could scarce have paid had I departed from Oxford, to which place they were, so to speak, necessarily bound. Their chief means of living came from the land that had been my father's at Eynsham, and was now by law descended to me. That most worthy man, John Vickers, paid them his rent (which he might easily have withheld) most honourably, not waiting indeed for set seasons, but coming into the city on market days, or during the siege, whenever occasion offered, and paying, as he thought they might have need. God reward him for his truth and kindness! There were those that called him trimmer and turncoat and such ill-names, because he was friendly with them that were in power. But I say that if all men of England had been as true to what they saw of right and duty, of which, indeed, some perceive more and some less, surely things had gone better with this realm than they did.

I therefore, and many others with me, for like reason, or others that had no less constraining power, tarried in Oxford, following our usual manner of life, and waiting for what might ensue. And, indeed, it mattered but little to me. My Scholarship was at the best but of small value, something less than three pounds by the year, and now was fallen to about thirty shillings from defect in the revenues of the College, of whose tenants some lacked the ability to pay (having had their farms wasted by the war), and some the will. Nor was I like to exchange it for any better preferment, being well known in my College and elsewhere as a zealous King's man. Having therefore so little to lose that the very scurviest and most beggarly knave under the sun would scarce have perjured himself to gain or to save it, I could abide the end with a calm mind; though, indeed, I do trust I had been no less constant had I had the best preferment in the University, the Deanery of Christ Church, to wit, or the President's place at Magdalen College. And I was further confirmed in this temper by the marriage of my sister Dorothy with Master William Blagrove, Bachelor of Divinity of St. John's College, that had lately succeeded to the vicarage of Enstone. 'Twas an old contract between Dorothy and Master Blagrove, being first entered into in the year 1641, and now completed about the space of a year after my father's death. Yet they thought themselves fortunate that the end was no longer delayed. (And indeed I could name a couple of lovers that were contracted for forty and three years, expecting all the while till a certain rectory should fall vacant.) Nevertheless it may be doubted whether delay had not served them better. 'Tis certain that they had no small share of that trouble in the flesh which St. Paul does prophesy to all them that were not content to abide single as he was. I doubt whether these prophecies, even in the mouth of an apostle, deterred many whose hearts were set on matrimony, and indeed it must be remembered there was gain as well as loss. But of Dorothy and her husband I shall have occasion to speak again. Meanwhile I may say so much, that she being happily married, if it be happiness to have a learned and virtuous husband but poor in this world's goods withal, and my mother going to live with her, I was left master of myself and free to act as might seem most expedient.

For a while it seemed as if nothing would be done, and some even began to hope that all things would be suffered to continue as they were. I indeed was not one of these, nor did I think that it would be well if it should be so. For, indeed, the University had almost ceased to be; there were few or none that lectured, and very few to hear, had teachers been ever so many; such as remained were much debauched by the loose companionship which they had taken up during the war; the colleges were half empty or rented out to laics lest they should altogether fall into ruin. It cannot be doubted therefore but that there was need of some visitation; nor was that which followed of a harsher sort than was to be looked for. 'Tis ever the rule in this world that it goes ill with the conquered, and the conquerors divide the spoil. I say not that there was no harshness used, nor none driven out that might have been kept, not only with advantage to the University, but without loss to the new rulers; but this only, that the victors bore themselves less haughtily and cruelly than might have been looked for, especially when it is considered what some of them had themselves suffered.

And now to speak of what was done. In the month of May, in the year 1647, came the visitors to Oxford, twenty-four in number, though of these not a few were content from the beginning to stand aloof from the business,

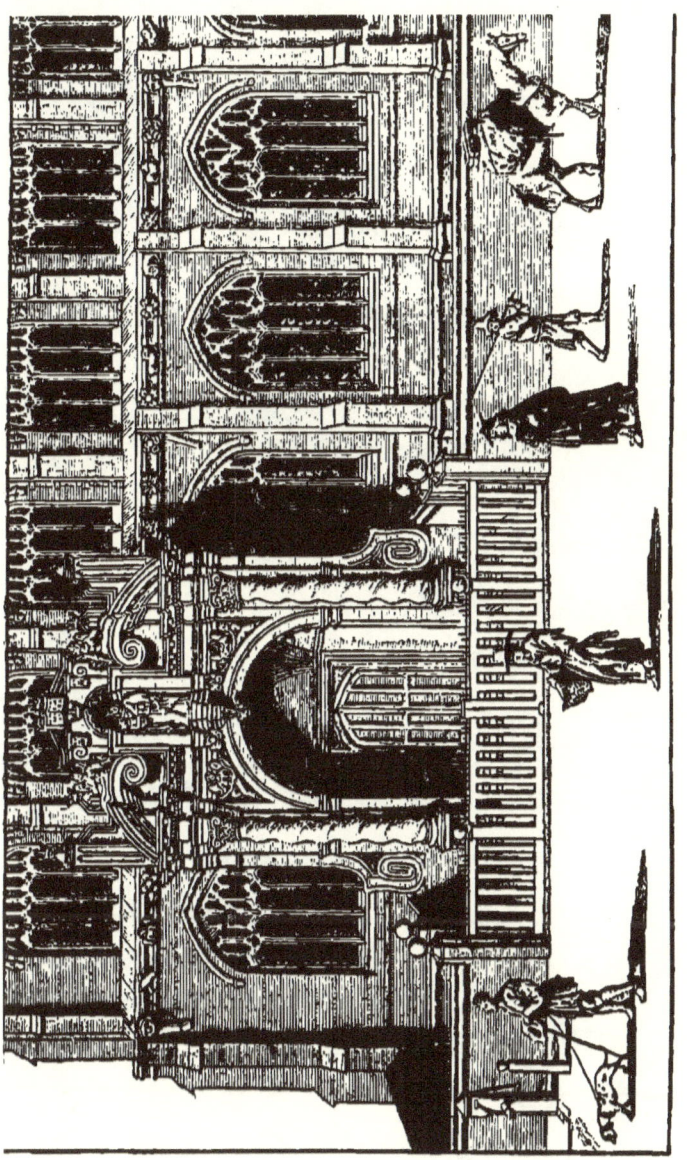

The Porch of St. Mary's Church, Oxford.

leaving it to the management of the clerics. They made but an ill beginning of their work. First, they delayed their coming over long after their appointment, and this they did because the Parliament soldiers in Oxford, vexed at certain grievances they had in respect of their pay and other matters, made a mutiny, so that they feared to show themselves. And next, on the day which they had appointed for the University to appear before them, which was the fourth day of June, they themselves failed of their time. Their citation to the Vice-Chancellor, Doctors and Masters was, "You shall appear before us between nine and eleven of the clock in the forenoon of the day aforesaid." So the Vice-Chancellor with the others assembled duly in the Convocation House. But the visitors went to St. Mary's Church, where, after prayers, there was a sermon preached by Master Robert Harris, of Magdalen Hall, who was one of them. But Master Harris, being full of his office, and having much to say concerning the iniquities of the prelatical party and the like things, was more than ordinary long in his discourse.

When, therefore, the clock struck eleven and the visitors were not yet come, Master Vice-Chancellor leaves the house, the bedels with their staves, as the custom is, walking before. And it so chanced that at this very time the visitors were about to enter. Then cries the bedel, a bold fellow that was afterwards resolute not to give up his staff, "Room for Master Vice-Chancellor;" to whom the visitors, being thus taken unawares, gave place. As they passed, Master Vice-Chancellor very civilly moved his cap to them, saying, " Good-morrow, gentlemen, 'tis past eleven of the clock," and so passed on, nor took any further heed of them.

'Twould be tedious to relate all the hindrances that after this were put in their way, how their notices and citations were torn down so soon as they were put up, and the books which they called for were not delivered up, so that, what with opposition from without, and divisions within (the Independents now having the great power and being minded to thrust down the Presbyterians from the first place), nothing was done. Nay, though

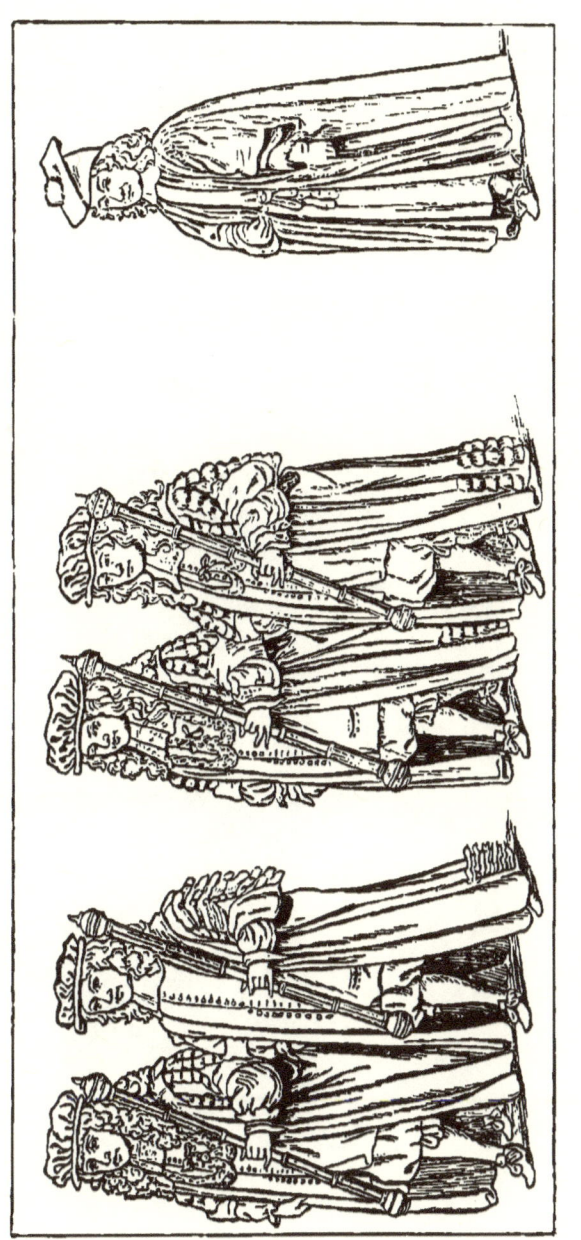

The Vice-Chancellor preceded by the Esquire Bedells.

my Lord Pembroke, that was Chancellor of the University, came down in his own person, and stormed at the Vice-Chancellor, telling him with many oaths (in which he was said to be proficient beyond all men of his time), that the devil had raised him to that office, and that it was fit that he should be whipped, nay, hanged; even so they made no progress. Nor could they gain possession of the keys of the University, for these the clerks obstinately kept (as for the register they took it by force from the Registrar's room) and the gold and silver staves were, as I have said, denied them, so that they were sadly shorn of the dignity which should have belonged to them. And this, I understand, vexed them as much as anything.

But at last, in the month of March, 1648—that is to say, nigh upon two years after the surrender of the city—the visitors did set to their work in earnest, and beginning with Magdalen College, demanded of every one whether he submitted to the authority of Parliament in this present visitation. And to this demand a plain answer was required. Truly it was piteous to see the straits to which honest men were reduced, that were loath to offend their conscience and yet would willingly have kept their means of livelihood. Some, especially among the cooks, butlers, porters, and other servants of the College, pleaded that they were ignorant and unlearned, and did not rightly understand how to answer that which was demanded of them. And some of the younger sort pleaded their tender age why they should not answer so hard a question. Others, again, hedged themselves in with sundry conditions and reservations, if by any means they could satisfy both their own consciences and the visitors. Here I have transcribed some of the answers.

"I am not of the understanding (my years being so tender) to hold your thesis which you propose, either affirmative or negative."

"Whereas very learned and judicious men have desired time, I shall think it presumption in me to answer it extempore."

"It is beyond my weak apprehension to give you any positive answer."

"My weak capacity cannot resolve you of this so hard a question."

"I submit in all cases not exempted by oath."

"I submit so far as my oath giveth me leave."

"When I shall be satisfied in conscience that I may lawfully do it, I will willingly submit."

"I do submit to King and Parliament in this visitation, so far as lawfully I may."

"I do not conceive that this visitation doth at all concern me."

"Whereas" (this was made by a gentleman of Christ Church) "I, being a Commoner here, do receive no benefit from the House, but living at great expense, and daily expecting to be taken home by my friends, I think this visitation doth not concern me."

"Sirs, to acknowledge the authority of Parliament in this visitation were to acknowledge you lawful visitors, and to acknowledge you lawful visitors were to say more than I know; and also to acknowledge many visitors, whereas I can but acknowledge one."

For myself I rather admired such answers as were given by Francis Dixon and Joseph Carricks, students of Christ Church, whereof the one said:

"I, Francis Dixon, shall not submit to any visitors but the King, and do acknowledge no visitor but the King."

And the other:

"I, John Carricks, will not submit to the visitation; I will not."

And, indeed, the reservations of the others served them but little, for the visitors shut them at last to a plain "Yes" or "No."

On the seventh day of May came the visitors to Lincoln College, and set us the same question. The greater part submitted; these I name not, nor say that they sinned against their conscience. There is One that judgeth, to whom they shall answer. As for me, I met the visitors with a plain "No," and having before, as knowing what should follow, prepared all things against my departure, left Oxford that very same day.

CHAPTER XVI.

OF MY KINSFOLK AT ENSTONE.

My sister Dorothy and her good husband, Master Blagrove, had long been earnest with me that I should visit them; and this, though there was that which drew me elsewhere, I now purposed to do, both because I desired to see my kindred again and to learn how they fared, and because Enstone was of a convenient nearness to Oxford. Such goods as I had I put in charge of a worthy citizen, Master Mallam, a draper, that had his dwelling in the Cornmarket, a good man that loved the King and the Church in his heart, but bare him so discreetly that he had the favour of the opposite faction. My books, which were indeed my chief possessions, though these also were neither many in number nor of great price, I gave into the charge of Anthony Wood, that was Bible-clerk of Merton College (which place though a King's man he had kept by the special favour of Sir Nathaniel Brent, the Warden of the said College). This Anthony was a great lover of books, and studious beyond his years, of which he at that time numbered about sixteen. These matters settled, I, taking with me only so much as I could conveniently carry on my back, and with a stout walking-staff in my hand—such as the good Bishop Jewel did lend to Master Richard Hooker, pleasantly calling it his horse—set out on my journey, which, being twenty miles or thereabouts, I accomplished in the space of six hours. I found a pleasant company gathered at Master Blagrove's house, for he had that day christened his little son, so that my coming was in season. After the first greeting, says my sister Dorothy to me:

"Now, Philip, kiss your godson; though indeed you are but a negligent godfather. Had you but come six hours sooner you had answered for yourself. As it is you must thank Master Willis here, whom I must now make known to you, for standing in your place."

"Nay, Dorothy," I answered, "you cannot rightly blame me. No man could have done to-day's business more speedily than I. This very morning, mind you, come the visitors to Lincoln College, and, my betters disposed of, call me before them. 'Philip Dashwood,' says the chief among them, Sir Nathaniel Brent, that is warden of Merton College, 'do you submit to this visitation?' 'Sirs,' said I, 'I do not submit.' 'Then you are expelled,' says the great man; and, turning to the clerk, 'Take a note of his name and sentence;' and to the manciple, 'Strike out his name from the books;' and having waited till I saw it done, I even turned on my heel, and so departed without a word. I warrant that my business filled not more than three minutes at the most. And this was scarce ten hours ago, for the visitors came to us about eight of the clock."

When I had told them my tale, my sister Dorothy, who had ever a tender heart, and thought better of me than I deserved, cried out:

"That was well, my brave Philip. I cannot be patient with the time-serving knaves who would keep their preferment at cost of their faith."

"Nay, Dorothy," said I, "mine was but a small matter, a few shillings by the year, which, in the common course, I could not have had much longer. 'Twas easy enough to give up so small a thing, but I judge not them who for wife and children's sake have strained their conscience, it may be, beyond that which is right."

As I spake, I noticed that my good brother looked somewhat grave and heavy, and so went on—

"But *cras seria*, as some one hath it, which may be translated, Mistress Dorothy, lest, haply, you have forgotten your Latin, 'business to-morrow.' And now, Dorothy, tell me about this little Philip."

Dorothy had much to say about the babe, which I will not here set down. And when she had ended her talk, which she did, not because she had said enough concerning his beauty and goodness, but because she was constrained to depart with him and lay him in his cradle, from which he had been kept overlong, we discoursed about other things, as sport and country matters of divers kinds, buying and selling of horses and cattle and the like, with

Master Willis, who was a farmer, and a person of no small consideration, seeing that he paid more tithes than any other in the parish, and was churchwarden to boot. He was in a complaining mood, for which, doubtless, he had at the time sufficiently good reason, but which seems to be common to all who follow his occupation. I suppose that they who spend their time in this business of tilling the earth have ever from day to day disappointments, unseasonable weather, promise of crops ill performed, and the like, which, though they be severally small, yet from their number and frequent occurrence worry the soul; and it is ever the way with men that little evils obscure and drive out of mind great goods.

"It has ever been a poor life with us farmers, and now it is like to be poorer still. As for sport, there is scarce a hare or a partridge in the whole country side. For that the soldiers have taken good care. There was no odds between King's men and Parliament's men. One was as keen after these things as another, and what one chanced to leave the other was sure to take. And as for merrymaking, there is little of it left, and will soon be none. Why, 'tis a sin in the eyes of these sour-faced whining folk to eat a mince-pie; and as for baiting a bear or a bull, as has ever been done here till these bad times, we should be taken to prison for the very mention of such a thing. But these be strange times, sir. Why, our good parson himself, Master Blagrove here, if I may make bold to say so much to his face, has new-fangled fancies about such things. You would scarce believe it, sir, but he will not suffer the scholars to have their cock-throwing on Shrove Tuesday. I was wont to give the bird—some tough old fellow that was become too savage, as they will, sir, when they get past their age—and the master would tie him to a stake when school was ended for the morning, and the scholars, or such of them as had been diligent at their learning, would stand in a ring round about him and throw staves at him, and the lad that gave him the mortal blow ('twas strange to see how long a bird would live) would have a shilling for himself. Then comes Master Blagrove, and talks of cruelty and the like. Now, if a man deals barbarously with a Christian, I call him cruel; but why should we care about brute beasts that, as St. Peter has it, are 'made to be taken and destroyed?'"

Perceiving that Master Willis was getting to be somewhat warm on this matter, I rose from my place and said to my host: "I am somewhat weary, and, with your good leave, will to bed." On this signal the others also went their way.

The next day I rose betimes, and seeing my brother pacing to and fro in his garden made haste to join him.

"Philip," said he, "your dear sister is a very lioness for courage, though she is gentle also and loving. I have heard tell of wives that for fear of poverty for them whom they love, have tempted their husbands to compliance with base things. Verily your sister is not one of these. She would starve, yea and see her babe starve—which, I take it, would trouble her a hundredfold more—before she would let one false word pass her lips. And I do believe in my soul that if, which God forbid, I should yield to evil for her sake and the babe's (for I could not be so base as to yield to it for my own), she would leave me sooner than have a share in the unclean thing. And being so set in her mind, and resolved what she will do, she keeps such a cheerful mind as I cannot pretend to. And, indeed, to speak the whole truth, which I scarce like to do in her hearing, 'tis a dismal prospect. Hitherto, it is true, I have been marvellously protected. My good friend Sir Thomas Chesham, who is the principal man in this part, having both a freehold of his own and a very profitable lease from the College, has stood by me, so that while others have been dispossessed of their livings, both on my right hand and my left, I remain unharmed. 'Tis true there are murmurings against me; yea, and threats openly made. Once and again have my enemies come into the church, resolved, I doubt not, had they not been hindered, to drag me from my very pulpit. 'Twas the Sunday before Easter this very year that three troopers, with their swords by their side, came, having with them a preacher in a black gown, whom they would have put in my place. When I went up to the pulpit to preach, up starts one of the troopers, and would have left his place; but Sir Thomas rose from his seat and said,

'William Ball, and you, Hugh Peters, (for I know you both), you shall answer for this day's uproar. Master Blagrove is a good man, and has not been dispossessed by any sentence of law or commission. Till he be so, he, and he only, has a right where he is, and verily so long as I am master in this parish he shall keep it.'

"After that they were content to remain in their place, and I gave the Doctor such a screed of doctrine as, I warrant you, he had not heard for a long time. You see, Sir Thomas is a man of no mean authority, having been ever on the Parliament's side from the very beginning of these troubles. He was with Master Hampden in the Ship Money matter, and has served the cause with money and otherwise, having indeed raised no small part of a troop of horse from this very place. I would he had been otherwise minded; but if it had been so he could not have served me. Nor do I know how much longer his protection will avail. For I hear, and that from the good man himself, that he is ever in less and less accord with them that have now the chief authority. He would gladly have made peace with the King and set him again on his throne, with due provision made for liberty; nor does he hold with those that cry out for a Republic. And in religion he is a Presbyterian, yet of such a sort that he is not ill-content to live under a Bishop so that he have no Popish ways. But as you know, brother Philip, these are not the opinions which find favour in high places in these days, and I know not how soon he may find even himself in danger."

"And what will you do, Master Blagrove?" for so I was wont to call him in consideration of his age, which was, I suppose, the double of mine at this time.

"I shall wait," answered he; "and when I am dispossessed suffer it with what patience I may. I have not the spirit of my good neighbour, Master Warden, of Haythrop; for when they would have intruded a new minister into his house he would not give place, but declared himself resolved not to give up his house to the usurper but with his life. Accordingly he caused his bed to be brought down into his parlour, kept his gun still charged, and had a watch set all night. Ay, and so bravely and constantly did he bear himself that the usurper had to betake himself elsewhere till Master Warden's death, which indeed happened but a few weeks since, he being then in his eighty-seventh year. He was a stout fellow, and his people loved him, for never man had a more open hand. But 'tis in my temper to yield more peaceably; for I have given pledges to Fortune, whereas Master Warden had been many years a widower, and his children had long since grown up, and gone forth into the world. But come, let us talk of other things. '*Sufficient unto the day is the evil thereof.*'"

I was yet bound by my promise to Sir Thomas Fairfax (now become by his father's death Lord Fairfax) that I would not bear arms against the Parliament, the three years for which this said promise held good running until the fourteenth day of June, on which day, it will be remembered, the battle of Naseby was fought. But for this 'tis very like that I had taken part with His Majesty's friends who in this year sought to raise the kingdom on his behalf. This they did in many diverse parts, as in Wales, where certain officers that had lately fought against the King now took up arms for him, and in Essex where my Lord Capel with others held Colchester in his name; nor were they without good hope of success, the Scots being ready to help, and the fleet also setting their officers aside and submitting them to the Prince of Wales. It was well for me that things were otherwise ordered, for, as is well known, all these beginnings ended in nothing. As for myself, when I was free from my promise (which was about a month after my coming to Enstone), I tarried where I was, judging that my duty kept me there. For first my mother was very urgent with me that I should stay. "His Majesty is a kind prince," she would say, "and now that I have lost my husband in his cause, will not ask from me my son also." Also I felt myself bound in kindness to my sister and her husband, that had relieved me in my need, and were now, I could perceive, in no small need of such help as I could give. For Master Blagrove, for lack of a tenant, had been constrained to farm his own glebe, which glebe was indeed the main support of his living. But what could a man do in such a business who, I do verily believe, knew not a plough from a harrow, or barley from wheat? Books on husbandry he had none, save you may reckon as such Hesiod's *Works and Days*, and the *Georgics* of Virgil; nor, had he possessed the wisest treatises that have ever been writ, may a man get any great benefit from that which is written. And as for buying and selling, there was never a man in this world so incapable of doing these to his own profit. I have noted that 'tis always hard for gentlefolk to hold their own in the market, be they ever so shrewd and full of knowledge. But my brother, being as simple as he was good, would sell his goods for the price, be it ever so small, that was first offered to him, and would buy for whatever was asked. Here, then, I found excellent occasion to serve him and my mother and sister also, who had otherwise fared but ill. Of farming I knew somewhat, having learnt it from my father, who was himself, as I have said, well acquainted with it; and as for dealings in the market, though I doubt not I was sometimes circumvented (for your rustic, look he ever so simple, is more than a match in cunning for your townsman), yet I took good care that he should not suffer any grievous wrong. And when the harvest was ended, I journeyed to Northamptonshire to see good Master Ellgood and my sweet Cicely. And there, for the land about Naseby is high and cold so that the seasons are later by far than in Oxfordshire, I was able to do service to the good man in the gathering of his corn. 'Twas a happy time indeed, for I would ply the sickle, and she, not being one of those delicate maidens that can but sit at home with their embroidery, came after me, binding the sheaves, one Gilbert Davenant, a young lad from Rugby School, helping. And when the gathering in was finished we took holiday. Sometimes we had a party at bowls (which game, as I have said, the good man liked much, taking pains beyond measure to keep his green smooth). Then Cicely and I would take sides against her father and Gilbert; in this sport I had no small skill, having followed it much at Oxford, where are bowling greens as fair and smooth as any in this kingdom; and it was my delight to bring my sweet Cicely's bowl as near as might be to the jack, for so they call the mark whereat the players aim, driving it in at sacrifice of my own, or driving off her adversaries. And we came by practice to use this alliance to such good purpose that her good father and his companion could scarce win a rubber. It must be confessed that he would sometimes lose his patience and grow angry over the game (but on grave matters I never saw his anger stirred, though indeed he had suffered no small provocation). Now and then also she would walk with me to Naseby field, when I would rehearse to her all that I knew about the battle —a tale which she was never weary of hearing. Sometimes also we would angle in the Nen, which river, though here but a petty stream, flowed but a little way eastward from her father's dwelling. It was a happy time, such as I had never before enjoyed, but it was soon to be broken through by a most grievous interruption.

CHAPTER XVII.

OF MY GOING TO LONDON.

In the latter part of the month of September I went for a while to Enstone, and having set things in order concerning the autumn sowings of corn and other matters which need to be looked to at that season of the year, and having also found by recommendation of John Vickers an honest man who should serve my brother as bailiff, I returned to Naseby about the first day of November.

Two or three days thereafter, as I sat in Master Ellgood's study reading Master Hooker's *Ecclesiastical Polity* (for I was preparing myself, so far as time and other circumstances permitted, for the taking of Holy Orders), comes Cicely knocking at the door and, opening it before ever I could speak, cries, "O Philip, see, John has come," and therewith brings in a fair youth, some two years older than herself, as I judged, and save that he had some four inches more of stature, of a singular likeness to her; and straightway on seeing him the doubt that had ever been in my mind whether I had ever before encountered him was resolved, for I perceived in a moment of time that the youth was the same that had yielded himself prisoner to my father at Copredy Bridge. As for him, he had no remembrance of me, at which indeed I did not wonder, considering what he had suffered that day. I doubted at the first whether I should make myself known to him, thinking, not without good reason, that he had no cause to love me. But the better thought prevailed that I should be honest before all things, nor endure to have some secret hanging, as it were, over my head and ever ready to fall; and indeed I had made confession to Cicely of my savagery in this matter and had received absolution from her. So I said:

"Master Ellgood, we have met before."

And when he regarded me steadfastly, yet without any sign of knowing me, I said, "Do you remember one Dashwood at Copredy Bridge?"

"Ay," said he, "as gallant a gentleman as ever sat on horseback. He saved me when I was in no small peril of my life, and gave me as courteous treatment as prisoner ever had, and settled for me my exchange, so that my captivity had scarce begun when it was ended. I hope that he is in good health and prosperity. But you are not he; you must be younger by a score of years at the least."

"He was my father," said I, "and I would fain shelter myself under his name, for, as for me, you have small cause to thank me."

And I made my confession to him. When I had finished he stretched out his right hand to me with a great laugh, saying:

"Why make such ado? There was no harm done. And if you had made an end of me I do not know that anyone would have been the loser, save, as they pleased to think, my good father and Cicely here; and, indeed, I had not lived to see such evil days as these. Know you the last tidings?"

"No," said I; "I have heard nothing, save that the Lieutenant-General Cromwell has trodden the King's friends under foot everywhere. But in truth I have been thinking of other things."

Thereat I blushed, which is a foolish trick that I have, and Cicely also blushed for company. Then John Ellgood, looking from one to another, saw something of what was between us. I know not that any man has at the first a particular kindness to him whom his sister favours (which is indeed a mighty ungrateful thing, for the lover has always a singular affection for his mistress's brothers), but being a good lad and of a kind heart he said nothing, only I thought that I heard him say to himself, "Is this a time——," and so brake off. "Well," he said, after he had been silent awhile, "listen to me. Four years ago we were enemies, now, I doubt not, we are friends." (This I was mightily glad to hear, fearing what might befall my love for Cicely.) "I fought for the Parliament—thinking that they had the better cause —against the King, and I yet believe, though here, doubtless, you agree not with me, that I was in the right. But 'tis otherwise with me now; and, indeed, 'tis not now the Parliament, but the Army, that reigns, and the Lieutenant-

General Cromwell and his fellows seek not the redressing of wrongs and securing of liberties, but the setting up of a new rule; and because they know in their hearts that this cannot be firmly established so long as the King stands in the way, though he be a prisoner and helpless, therefore they are minded to bring him to judgment for what they are pleased to call his treasons against this nation, and having so brought him—'tis almost too horrible to say, yea, even to think—to put him to death."

Since then this thing has been done, and done with approval from some that are undoubtedly pious and learned persons (though I doubt not that the greater part of the nation abhorred the act), so that it has become in a way familiar, but then (I speak of myself and of many others) it had not been so much as thought of. That the King might suffer much at the hand of his enemies; that he might even be slain by some wicked or fanatic persons, as kings before him—Richard, the second of the name, to wit, and Henry the Sixth—had been slain by secret violence, I had deemed to be probable; but that he should be brought to trial with accustomed forms of law and justice, and having been so brought, should be publicly and in the face of day put to death, seemed too horrible to be believed. There had never happened such a thing before, save only—and let no one judge it to be profane that this was the first thought of many—save only when our Lord Himself was condemned by Pilate and crucified.

"It cannot be," I said; "no men could dare to be so impiously wicked."

"Nay," said he, "'tis but too true. But they shall not have their way without hindrance, for, besides many that have been the King's friends from the beginning, there are some who, as I myself, were against him at the first, and so feel the more bound, as having contributed to his present low estate, to help him in his present necessity. But we will talk more of these things when my father shall return."

Master Ellgood had ridden to Harborough that day on some business that he had.

He being returned after supper, Cicely also being present, John Ellgood set forth to him what I have written down above, and this also, that there were many of the same way of thinking with himself, and that they purposed to assemble in London so that they might be in readiness against whatever might happen, watching above all things for some occasion to save the King out of the hands of his enemies. When he had ended Master Ellgood the elder said:

"I had hoped that you had done with strife. Yet I would not say a word to keep you back. I hold not, indeed, with them who say that a king can do no wrong, and that we be bound to yield him obedience in all things without question. That we may lawfully restrain him by force from breaking down our liberties I do heartily believe, but I am persuaded that we cannot rightfully bring him to judgment; for, indeed, what authority is there that is competent for such things? And, again, shall there be no end to the shedding of blood? If this, indeed, be done 'twill do more damage to true liberty than the King's victory had done. Therefore, John, I bid you God's speed on your errand; and you, too, Philip, if you are minded to go with him."

Thereat I, sitting, as was my wont, by Cicely, and holding her hand in mine, felt it tighten upon mine; and looking at her, I saw her flush and grow pale, as was her wont when she was much moved.

"Nor would I stay you," she whispered, "though I, too, had hoped that all these things were finished and done with."

It was concluded, therefore, that night that we should go; but that there was no present need to depart. But it was needful that I should go for awhile to my brother at Enstone, and this without delay, and returned to Master Ellgood's home about the twentieth of November. Then again eight days after we set out for London and came thither on the second day of December, and found a lodging with my kinsman Rushworth, of whom I have written in the relation of my school days. The next day, being Sunday, we worshipped at the chapel of the Savoy, where Dr. Thomas Fuller preached the sermon; a most learned, witty, and eloquent discourse, and marvellously bold—the condition of the kingdom, wherein the King's enemies were supreme, being considered. His text was 1 Samuel xv. 22. "*For rebellion is as the sin of witchcraft;*" which he enforced with much plainness of speech, so that I marvelled that he was neither presently hindered from speaking nor afterwards visited. But the good Doctor is no respecter of persons, for did he not, being appointed preacher by the Parliament, discourse before them on these words (spoken by Mephibosheth to David concerning Ziba): "*Yea let him take all, so that my lord the King come again in peace,*" to their no small discontent?

The day following we went to the House of Commons, being bestowed by favour of one of the ushers under one of the galleries. 'Tis a noble chamber, and the circumstances of the assembly, the Speaker, for example, with his mace, majestic; but itself, methinks, scarce a match in dignity for its surroundings, the members sitting for the most part as if they cared nought for that which was being done, so loudly did they talk with each other and laugh; but if one of greater note rose to speak there was straightway silence. As for us, we listened with all our ears, and that for many hours, for the House, meeting at ten of the clock in the forenoon, prolonged its sitting till nine of the clock in the morning of the day following, nor did we, save for refreshment's sake for a few minutes, leave our place. It was a marvellous strange scene, for sometimes it would seem as if all the House were asleep, some one speaking of whom none took any heed; then again there would be almost a tumult, angry crying out and stamping with the feet, so that one had almost thought the members ready to fly at each other's throats. And above the great torches flared, making a mighty smoke and heat, so that though the air outside was cold and frosty, within the heat was like to suffocate. At the last, all being wearied out (and some of the older sort had been long asleep), the House came to a division, the question being one that touched the late conferences with the King, and the resolution to be determined being this: "That the King's concessions to the Parliament are sufficient grounds for settling the peace of the kingdom." And this resolution was carried by the majority of voices, the Ayes being one hundred and twenty, and the Noes fifty.

Thereupon we went to our lodging with great joy, and found Master Rushworth waiting for us, who somewhat dashed our spirits.

"Ah!" said he, "'twould be well if the Parliament were our masters; but 'tis not so. The power is not in Mr. Speaker's mace, but in the Lord General's sword, or, rather, for 'tis said that the Lord General's day is past, with Master Cromwell and his colonels. I little thought that I should ever desire more power for the Parliament; yet so I do, for verily the Army will be a worse master."

The next day we were again early at the House, and Master Usher, who seemed to have some knowledge beforehand of what should happen, put us in a place in the lobby. We noted coming in that the guards of the Houses had been changed; for, whereas on the day before there had stood about the doors and passages the City Trainbands, very gaily accoutred, with their clothes and arms bearing no stain of war, there were now in their place two regiments of soldiers, that were manifestly veterans of many campaigns.

And now we, standing behind in the shadow,

for we did not desire to be espied, see some soldiers by the place of entering into the House of Commons, one of them, who seemed to be in command, having a paper in his hand.

"Mark you that man," whispered the Usher in my ear; "'tis Colonel Pride. Be sure that he has not come for nought."

And indeed it was so, for so soon as a member came to the door the said Colonel would turn round; now to a gentleman that stood by his side (whom I understood to be my Lord Grey of Groby), and now to one of the doorkeepers, and would ask his name, and if he were on the list, then he seized upon him and delivered him to one of the soldiers, who led him off. All save one departed quietly; and he, whom I knew to be Master William Prynne, one of the visitors that had come from the Parliament to Oxford, made as if he would have drawn his sword; thereupon the Colonel called for a guard of soldiers (and indeed both the Court of Requests and the stairs, and the lobby were filled with them), at the sight of whom Master Prynne yielded himself quietly. We saw thus seized by Colonel Pride and his soldiers forty and one members. Thus we were persuaded that nothing was to be hoped in the King's favour from the Parliament, were their will ever so good. Thereafter, indeed, all that had been zealous for a reconciliation being, as the extreme men were pleased to say, purged from the House, it voted nothing but what was agreeable to the will of the Army.

I shall not here set down in particular how we employed ourselves during the month that now followed, not knowing but what this writing may fall into unfriendly hands, for though I am not careful to conceal my own opinions and actions, I should be loath to entangle others in my dangers. Let it suffice then to say that we busied ourselves in devising means by which we might deliver the King out of the hands of his enemies, and that in so doing we both found help where we looked not for it, and found it not where we had most expected it. For some that were imagined to be the King's enemies were now earnest on his behalf, and some that professed themselves to be his friends were lukewarm, ay, and worse. Meanwhile we were diligent in attending at the debates of the

Commons' House, though, indeed, there was but little debating when a man might lose his liberty for any freedom of speech; and so watched without ceasing for what turn matters should take.

CHAPTER XVIII.

OF THE TRIAL OF THE KING.

On the twenty-eighth day of December, we, being according to our wont in the Commons' House, heard read the report of a Committee to which had been committed the matter of the King's trial. It ran thus, to put it in a few words, that "Charles Stuart" (for so they entitled his gracious Majesty) "had acted contrary to his trust in setting up his standard and making war against the Parliament;" and this report was debated on the day following, and it was resolved that he should be tried on this same charge, and to the same Committee was given the business of choosing who should be his judges.

This same day there happened a thing which showed of how resolute and fierce a temper were they who had the chief power at this time. We had had some converse with one Pitcher, that had been a major in the King's army and was then lying hid in London, being intent indeed on the same business with which we were occupied. We counselled him to depart, for indeed his life was already forfeit. He had been in the King's garrison at Worcester, and had engaged not to bear arms any more against the Parliament. Nevertheless, he had been found in arms in the late fighting at Pembroke. And having been yet again spared on condition that he should depart from this realm, nor return thither for the space of two years without leave first had, he still delayed in London. I told him that it was a desperate matter, and that he had best depart; but he was obstinate to remain. " Nay," said he, " who can say what will happen in the space of two years, even to the doing of his gracious Majesty to death? There I can avail nothing; here, perchance, I may do some good. Though it may be but the thousandth part of a chance, I will even risk my life upon it." And this he did, even to the losing of it. How it fell out I know not, whether one that saw him at Worcester or Pembroke knew him again, or whether he betrayed himself—for he was ever bold, even to rashness, in his speech —but 'tis certain he was taken at a tavern in Westminster, and the next day shot in St. Paul's Churchyard. I cannot name them that did it; but it was proof, if indeed proof were needed, that they who sought to help the King carried their lives in their hands.

On the first day of January the Commons' House voted that the King had been guilty of high treason in levying war against the Parliament.

The same night John Ellgood and I, walking near to Charing Cross, saw a mighty strange sight which was as a comedy in the midst of a tragedy. There met us a company of soldiers, and with them a whole *posse* of players, habited in their robes, as kings, and judges, and queens, and as the other characters that are wont to be seen upon the stage. We heard that the Lord General had commanded this to be done, and that the players still performing their plays against the ordinance of Parliament, the soldiers had taken them as they were from Drury Lane and Salisbury Court.

On the fourth day of January, the Lords

having rejected the ordinance concerning the trial of the King, the Commons declared that whatsoever was passed by them had the force of law, and this they did without any man saying " Nay!"

On the ninth day of the same month we, being in Westminster Hall (for we were always intent to see and hear what might happen), saw the Serjeant-at-Arms, bearing the mace upon his shoulder, having certain officers with him and six trumpeters, and a guard of horse and foot, ride into Westminster Hall and there proclaim, " If any man has aught against Charles Stuart, King of England, let him come before the Commissioners appointed for the trial of the said Charles Stuart at this time to-morrow and make it known."

At length, on the nineteenth day of January, the trial was indeed begun, taking place in Westminster Hall, at the upper end, where the Courts of Chancery and King's Bench were wont to be held, the two courts being thrown into one for the greater convenience of the numbers that were likely to be assembled. And on this same day of the month they brought His Majesty from Windsor to the Palace of St. James, guarding him with no small care against a rescue, which, indeed, they had no small reason to fear.

It was permitted to all to enter the place of sitting, but the Hall and all the approaches thereto were very strongly kept with soldiers. John Ellgood and I attended this day and daily afterwards, having short swords and pistols under our cloaks, that we might be ready for any occasion that might arise; but our hopes were daily diminished, for though there were many that misliked the whole business, the dread of the army was upon them, and they dared not so much as stir a finger. Nevertheless, when men were content to sit in silence, yet there was a woman that had courage to speak out her mind, for when the list of Commissioners was read aloud, and the Crier gave forth the name of Thomas Lord Fairfax, being next after the name of the President of the Court, there was heard a voice, " He has more wit than to be here ; " and, afterwards, when (the impeachment being read aloud) the reader pronounced the words—" by the authority of Parliament and of all the good people of

England," the same voice spake again, "No, nor the hundredth part of them." Thereupon there was no small confusion; and it has been said by some that the officer of the guard commanded his men that they should fire upon the place from which this voice proceeded. But I heard no such order given, nor do I believe it; for who would dare thus to imperil the innocent along with the guilty? It was the Lady Fairfax, wife to the Lord General, that thus cried out. She was of the lineage of the Veres, an ancient house to whose honour her behaviour was conformable.

The next day the King was brought before the Court, and I, who had not seen him for nigh upon three years, noted that his aspect was somewhat changed, as, indeed, it might well be with his troubles. There was set for him a chair of crimson velvet, behind which there stood some thirty men, carrying halberds. The judges, of whom there were present some sixty (which was not the half of them that had been first named), sat in hat and cloak, the President wearing black. The King came in very stately, not moving his hat to the judges, but looking on them and on the spectators with a stern regard. Then, the crier having proclaimed silence, the President said:

"Charles Stuart, King of England, the Commons of England, being deeply sensible of the calamities that have been brought upon this nation, which are fixed upon you as the principal author of them, have resolved to make inquisition for blood;" and more to the same effect.

When the President had made an end, Master Coke, that was Solicitor for the Commonwealth, standing with two others upon the King's right hand, offered to speak. But the King, having a staff in his hand, laid it lightly upon his shoulder, as if he would bid him stay. This he did twice, and the second time the gold head of the staff dropped off, at which it was noted by some that were in the Court that the King manifestly changed colour.

Then the President ordered Master Solicitor to proceed, who said: "My Lord, I am come to charge Charles Stuart, King of England, in the name of the Commonwealth, and desire that the charge may be read," and so gave it to the Clerk. Thereat the King cried, "Hold;" nevertheless, the Clerk continuing to read, he sat down and so remained silent, till about the end, when he smiled, but looking very stern and severe. When the hearing was ended, the President said:

"Sir, the Court expects that you will make an answer to this charge."

Thereat the King answered: "I would know by what authority I am brought hither?"

PRESIDENT: "By authority of the people of England, whose elected King you are."

THE KING: "The kingdom of England has never been elective, but hereditary for near these two thousand years. I stand here more for the liberty of my people than do my pretended judges."

PRESIDENT: "'Tis well known how you have misused this trust. The Court must proceed."

THE KING: "I do not come as submitting to this Court. I was brought here by force. I see no House of Lords here; nor can there be a Parliament without a King."

Many times did the President command him

to answer, and he refused, saying that he should betray his trust in so doing. Thereupon he was remanded to St. James' Palace. As he went he pointed to the sword, which, with the mace, lay upon the table, and said, "I fear not that." There was a great shout as he walked down the Hall: "God save the King," and another, but not so loud, of "Justice, justice!" It is tedious to tell all that passed between the President and the King on the days following. Indeed, it was ever the same, the President desiring that the King should plead, and affirming that no prisoner could be suffered to deny the authority of the Court by which he was tried, and the King, on the other hand, being resolute to deny that he could be lawfully judged by them that pretended to do so. And this contention endured throughout three days. All that were present noted that the King, who commonly had a certain hesitancy in his speech, now spake with as much freedom as could be desired. At the last the President said:

"Sir, this is the third time that you have publicly disowned this Court, and put an affront upon it; how far you have preserved the privileges of the people, your actions have spoken it; and truly, Sir, men's intentions ought to be known by their actions; you have written your meaning in bloody characters throughout the whole kingdom. But, Sir, you understand the pleasure of the Court. Clerk, record the default; and, gentlemen, you that took charge of the prisoner, take him back again."

THE KING: "I will say this one word more to you; if it were my own particular, I would not say any more, nor interrupt you."

PRESIDENT: "Sir, you have heard the pleasure of the Court, and you are (notwithstanding you will not understand it) to find that you are before a court of justice."

On the fifth day of the trial, so called, and on the day following, the Court sat not in Westminster Hall, as before, but in the Painted Chamber, where they heard witnesses. John Ellgood and I were not present, access to the chamber not being so ready as to the Hall, but we heard that witnesses, two score and more in number, of all ranks and conditions, were examined, and testified to certain acts of war on the part of the King, beginning with the setting up of his standard at Nottingham, and proceeding through all parts of the late war. All this, methinks, was matter of common notoriety, and might conveniently have been spared.

On the seventh day of the trial, being the twenty-seventh of January, we were betimes in the Hall, which was crowded beyond all that had been before, all being now convinced that this great tragedy was drawing to an end. The President was in scarlet, having before been habited in black. His Majesty came in, covered as before, whereat some of the soldiers that were set on guard cried, "Justice! Execution!" He said:

"I desire a word to be heard, and I hope I shall give no occasion of interruption."

PRESIDENT: "You may answer in your time. Hear the Court first."

THE KING: "I desire to be heard, and 'tis only a word. A hasty judgment is not so soon recalled."

PRESIDENT: "You shall be heard before judgment is given."

The President then declared that the Court, having considered the crimes laid to the charge

Trial of the King.

of the prisoner, and found them to be proved, were agreed upon a sentence to be pronounced against him. But in respect that he doth desire to be heard before sentence be read and pronounced, the Court had resolved that they will hear him. Then, turning to the King, he said, "If that which you say be to question the Court's jurisdiction, you shall not be heard in it. But if you have anything to say in defence of the thing charged, the Court has given me a command to let you know they will hear you."

The King: "This many a day all things have been taken away from me, but that which is dearer to me than my life, which is my conscience and my honour. If I had respect to my life more than the peace of the kingdom, and the liberty of the subject, certainly I should have made a particular defence for myself."

After this he went on to ask that he might be permitted to say something to the Lords and Commons assembled in the Painted Chamber, to whom, he said, he had somewhat of no small import to say.

The Court withdrew to consider this, but returning in half-an-hour's time, the President said, "'Tis an excellent maxim in law 'Nulli negabimus, nulli vendemus, nulli deferemus justitiam.' There must be no more delay with you, Sir. We are now to proceed to sentence and judgment."

After more disputing of the same sort the President commanded silence. Which done, the Clerk read the sentence, which was: "Whereas the Commons of England have appointed a Court for the trial of Charles Stuart, King of England, and whereas a charge of high treason and other crimes was read, the Court doth adjudge that the said Charles Stuart, as a tyrant, traitor, murderer, and a public enemy, shall be put to death by the severing of his head from his body."

All the Court stood up to signify their assent.

THE KING: "Will you hear me a word, Sir?"

PRESIDENT: "Sir, you are not to be heard after sentence."

KING: "No, Sir?"

PRESIDENT: "No, Sir; by your favour, Sir. Guard, withdraw your prisoner."

KING: "By your favour, Sir, hold the sentence."

But when nothing availed he said: "I am

not suffered to speak. Expect what justice other people will have."

While His Majesty was being taken away by the guards, as he passed down the stairs, the soldiers scoffed at him, casting the smoke of their tobacco, which was very distasteful unto him, and blowing their pipes in his way; and as he passed there were some who cried, "Justice, justice!" to whom he said, "Poor soldiers, for a piece of money they would do so for their commanders." But all the soldiers, though they had the Parliament's pay, were not so minded; for one of them cried—but whether this day or another I know not—"God bless the King," and when his officer struck him with a a cane, the King said, "Methinks the punishment is greater than the offence."

CHAPTER XIX.

OF THE KING'S DEATH.

THE sentence of death on the King I had looked for, but that it would indeed be executed I could not believe. But when I said so much to John Ellgood I found that he thought otherwise.

"Philip," said he, " I have seen more of these men than you. Of those who stood in arms against the King many desire nothing more than to protect the liberties of this realm against him, or, if you would rather have it so, against his ill-counsellors. These at the first prevailed; but 'tis otherwise now. In civil troubles the more violent ever gain the upper hand. What befell the more moderate sort we saw with our own eyes when Colonel Pride and his men laid violent hands upon some fifty members of the House of Commons. They that now bear rule, of whom the Lieutenant-General Cromwell is the chief, are resolved to have no truce with kingship. Whether they seek the good of their country or their own aggrandisement I know not, but so it is. And they know full well that after the King's death, of truce or peace there can be no more talk. On this, therefore, they are steadfastly resolved."

"But the kings," I said, "the kings of France and Spain, will they suffer it?"

"I doubt," answered he, "whether they would so much as stir a finger to hinder it. But whether they would or no, there will be no time or space of action. Be sure that execution will follow sentence right speedily."

And so indeed it was. Before three days had passed since the pronouncing of the sentence, 'twas all finished. Of the kings, too, John Ellgood spake but too truly. Their ambassadors said not a word to hinder the King's death. Indeed, the only word of remonstrance came, not from a king, but from a republic, the States of the Dutch being, by their envoy, very earnest with the Parliament that they should not take the King's life.

As for our hopes of delivering His Majesty by force of arms or stratagem, they were at an end, so closely and strongly was the King guarded. Yet were we loath to depart, hoping even against hope to the very end that the people, ay, and the very soldiers, might rise against this monstrous deed.

Of that which I shall now write down, part I heard from the lips of Sir Thomas Herbert, who was gentleman of the body to the King, and indeed had been so from his first surrender by the Scots, and partly from a certain Doctor Farrer, a physician who stood very near to the scaffold.

This is the narration of Sir Thomas Herbert:

"For awhile after the King came to London he dined publicly in the Presence Chamber, and was served after the usual state—the carver, server, cup-bearer, and gentleman-usher attending and doing their offices—being given on the bended knee. But this was changed by command of the generals, and thereafter the dishes were brought up by soldiers; the cup was no longer given upon the knee. At first His Majesty was much discomposed, saying that no king had ever wanted such observance, and asking, 'Is there anything more contemptible than a despised prince?' But his remedy was to restrict his diet to as few dishes as possible, and to eat in private.

"Of the trial, if that mockery of justice may be so called, there is no need for me to speak. You yourselves saw it. You would hear of His Majesty's behaviour in private. On the day when sentence was pronounced, in the evening, the King gave me a ring from his finger ('twas an emerald set between two diamonds), and bade me go with it to a lady living in King Street, in Westminster (that I knew afterwards to be the King's laundress), and give it to her without saying anything. Being arrived at the lady's house I delivered her the ring. She took me into a parlour and there left me, and in a short while returned with a little cabinet that was closed with three seals. The next day, after prayers, which the Bishop had daily with the King, His Majesty broke the seals open and showed us what was contained in it; there were diamonds and jewels, for the most part broken Georges and Garters. 'You see,' said he, 'all the wealth now in my power to give to my two children.'

"The next day, being the twenty-ninth day of

January, came the Princess Elizabeth and the Duke of Gloucester her brother, to take farewell of the King their father, and to ask his blessing. The Princess, being the elder, was most sensible of her father's condition, as appeared by her sorrowful look and excessive weeping; and her little brother, seeing his sister weep, took the like impression. The King took them both upon his knees, and gave them his blessing, and admonished them of their duty to the Prince his successor and to their other relations. Then he gave them all the jewels, save the George that he wore, which was cut in an onyx with great curiosity, and was set about with twenty fair diamonds, and the like number on the reverse.

"That same day the Bishop of London preached before the King, taking for his text, Romans ii. 16: '*Of that day when God shall judge the secrets of men by Jesus Christ;*' and, after the sermon, continued with the King till it was some hours past dark.

"After the Bishop was gone to his lodging, the King continued two hours more in meditation and prayer. He then bade me sleep on a pallet by his bedside. I took small rest, but the King slept four hours, and awaking two hours before dawn opened his curtain to call me. And perceiving that I was disturbed in my sleep, for there was a light that burned all night, being a cake of wax set in a silver basin, he called me and bade me rise. 'For,' said he, 'I will get up, having a great work to do this day.' In a little while he said, 'This is my second marriage day; I would be as trim to-day as may be, for before night I hope to be espoused to my Lord.' He then appointed what clothes he would wear, and said, 'Let me have a shirt on more than ordinary, by reason that the season is so sharp as may probably make me quake. I would not have men think it fear. I fear not death. I bless God I am prepared.'

"Then I besought the King's pardon if I had been negligent in my service. After this the King delivered me his Bible, in the margin of which he had written annotations, and charged me to give it to the Prince. He also commanded me to give to the Duke of York his large ring sundial of silver, a jewel which he had much prized; and he gave commandment about sundry books to be given to diverse persons.

"After this I withdrew, and the King was for about an hour in private with the Bishop. The Bishop read to him, after prayers, the twenty-seventh chapter of St. Matthew's Gospel, which relates the passion of our Saviour. The King asked the Bishop if he had made choice of that chapter as being applicable to his present condition. The Bishop answered, 'May it please your gracious Majesty, it is the proper lesson for the day;' whereupon the King was much affected.

"After this Colonel Hacker knocked at the door, and, coming in, said in a trembling manner, ''Tis time to go to Whitehall, when your Majesty may have some further time to rest.' For a short while the King was private, afterwards he took the Bishop by the hand and said, 'Let us go;' and when he had passed through the garden into the park, he took from my hand a little silver clock, which he had bidden me carry, and gave it to me to keep in memory of him.

"There were several companies of horse and foot in the park, making a guard on either side as the King passed; and there was also a guard of halberdiers, some going before, and some following after; and the drums beat, making such a noise that one could hardly hear what another spoke.

"Being come to Whitehall the King passed into his bedchamber; and after prayer he bade me bring him some bread and wine, which being brought, the King broke the manchet and ate a mouthful of it, and drank a glassful of claret wine. After that I saw the King no more, for I could not bear to look upon the violence they would offer him upon the scaffold."

Here follows what I heard from Master Farrer :—

"The King seeing that his voice could not reach the people, spake what was in his mind to the gentlemen upon the scaffold, justifying himself for all that he had done, save for consenting to the death of my Lord Strafford, and forgiving his enemies. While he was speaking one of the gentlemen touched the edge of the axe, thereupon the King said, 'Hurt not the axe; that may hurt me.'

"The Bishop asked him that, for the world's satisfaction, he would say something of his affection for religion. The King said, 'I die a Christian according to the profession of the Church of England, as I found it left me by my father.' Then, turning to Colonel Hacker, he said, 'Take care that they do not put me to pain.' Also to a gentleman that came near the axe he said twice, with much earnestness, 'Touch not the axe.' Then, speaking to the executioner, he said, 'I shall say but very short prayers, and after that thrust out my hands.'

"The Bishop said, 'There is but one stage more. This stage is turbulent and troublesome, but you may consider it will carry you a very great way; it will carry you from earth to Heaven.'

"Then the King said, 'I go from a corruptible crown to an incorruptible, where no disturbance can be.'

"Then he took off his cloak and his George, giving his George to the Bishop, and said at

Execution of King Charles I.

the same time, 'Remember!' and this done, laid his head upon the block; and I noted that his eye was as quick and lively as ever I have seen it."

But what I myself saw and heard may be told in few words. The scaffold had been made against the wall of the Palace of Whitehall, by the banqueting chamber, and the King, coming through one of the windows of this same chamber, stepped upon it. It was hung about with black, and in the midst was a block and an axe, and by the block stood two men that had their faces covered with masks. A great number of soldiers stood about the scaffold, so that the people could not come near it; but the street and the tops of the houses and the windows were filled with such a multitude of people as I should think had scarcely before been gathered together. I could see the King speaking to them that were on the scaffold, and to the man that had the axe, and to the Bishop that stood by his side. After that I could see that he put his hair under his cap, for he had put a night-cap on his head, the headsman and the Bishop helping him. Then he knelt down, and laid his head upon the block. This done, there was silence for the space of about a minute, and the King stretched out his hands. Thereupon the headsman let fall the axe, which with one blow divided the head from the body. Then the other man that was masked took up the head by the hair, and cried out in a loud voice, "This is the head of a traitor!" to which all the people answered with such a dismal groan as was never heard before.

CHAPTER XX.

OF MATTERS AT ENSTONE.

How we felt, seeing the axe fall upon that sacred head, I shall not seek to write. We stood, as it were, astonished, looking, it may be, for vengeance to fall from Heaven on the city that had suffered such things to be done in its midst. After a while, when the people were now all dispersed, and the soldiers began to look as if they would question them that still tarried, we went very sadly to our lodging, and there debated between ourselves what it were best to do. Our errand in London was now at an end; nor had we the desire to tarry there any longer; and, indeed, so to do had imperilled our lives, or, at the least, our liberty. For it was manifest that they who had slain the King were determined to make an end of the business; and whom, indeed, having done such a deed, were they like to spare? I say not that they used their power with cruelty. 'Tis not so; rather they showed more mercy than could have been reasonably looked for. Yet this was afterwards to be proved; the danger for the present seemed imminent.

On the fourth day of February, therefore, John Ellgood and I departed from London, habited in Roundhead fashion for greater security of travelling. But there was no watch kept on them that would leave London, so we met with none to question us on our road. We travelled on foot, a mode that suited the slenderness of our purses, and also lent itself more readily to secrecy, for a man can hide himself when he cannot hide his horse; and on the third day came to our journey's end.

We found Dorothy and her husband in no little trouble; not yet, indeed, dispossessed but almost daily expecting so to be. At supper, Master Blagrove set forth to us how his affairs stood.

"I doubt," said he, "but that the end is well nigh come; and, indeed, I marvel, not without thankfulness, that it has been delayed so long:

'*Quem sors dierum cunque dabit lucro Appone,*' *

* " Reckon for gain whatever days Fate shall give thee."

as the poet Horace has it. And, indeed, I have had many days that have been denied to my neighbours. But for more I can, scarce hope. The good knight, my patron, is in disgrace with the powers that be, and can scarce keep himself out of prison, much less help his friends. Therefore, I am looking every day for a summons, and can but pray for God's grace to help me play valiantly a confessor's part."

And even while he was speaking his expectation was fulfilled, for there came a loud knocking at the door, and soon after a message brought into the parlour, which the little countrymaid could scarce deliver for fear, that a constable would speak with the parson.

"Let him come in hither," quoth my brother, whereupon the constable comes into the parlour. He was a rough fellow and given to some insolence of speech, but now he was civil enough, partly, may be, seeing he had to do with them that could presently chastise any liberty of speech; and partly, I do believe, because he was ashamed to show rudeness to so gracious a woman as was my sister Dorothy, and to Master Blagrove that was honoured both for courtesy and learning through the whole country side. He now delivered a brief to my brother, excusing his coming as a matter of necessity, and so, having first drunk a cup of ale to our health, which he did though 'twas against his principles, presently departed.

The brief summoned my brother to appear the day following at ten of the clock in the forenoon, at a tavern in Enstone, before certain Commissioners therein named, there to answer sundry charges made against his doctrine and manner of life. We had much talk about the matter, sitting up together till near upon midnight, but there was small comfort to be got concerning it, and I could see that my brother had no hope of a good ending.

The next day when he came back from the sitting of the Court (which was not till about three of the clock in the afternoon), he seemed somewhat more cheerful of aspect; but Dorothy crying to him, "Things, then, are better than you looked for," he said, "Nay, sweet love, 'tis only that I am easier in my mind, as a man will be, after long battling for life, when sentence has been pronounced, even though it be sentence of death. But hear my tale. As for the goodly list of Commissioners, 'twas, as I expected, all moonshine. There was not present one gentleman of birth and education. Timothy Fenn, the miller, whom they had chosen for their president, was as good a man as any; and Timothy, as you know, though passably honest, is not a shining light either for wit or knowledge. Others were rude fellows that could scarce put their names to a paper, and one or two had been to my knowledge in time past men of evil life; what they are I know not, but they were, I noted, especially bitter against me. But now for their doings. First, they examined me concerning doctrine. Were I to tell you what they said, what questions they asked, and in what way they received my answers, 'twould sound as a foolish jest. Let it suffice to say that there was not one that knew a word of Greek or even of Latin. When I quoted a few words of this last they took it as an affront, though it was but a common saw that every lawyer, and many a one that is no lawyer, has on the tip of his tongue. When I offered to prove that I had taught nothing but what was agreeable to Holy Scripture and the Fathers, they stopped me peremptorily. 'As for the Fathers, we desire to hear nothing of such papistical writers; but as for Scripture it is not you, but we that must be judges of what agrees thereto.' But these questions kept them but a little while; and, indeed, they were not at their ease in them.

"After this they proceeded to examine me about certain things in my life and conversation. I marvelled what charges would be brought against me, for, though I am not blameless, God knows, yet I have always walked soberly and discreetly, even denying myself in what I judged to be lawful recreations that I might not give offence to any; for I know that in these times any stick is good enough to beat a dog withal, especially if the dog be a poor parson.

"'We are credibly informed,' says Master President, 'that you have been seen coursing hares on the Sabbath day. What say you to this?'

"For a while I could say nothing, having no remembrance of anything that could be made to bear such a colour; but at the last I remembered something that might by great malice and ingenuity be so interpreted. My brother going abroad after Naseby fight, gave me a greyhound to keep, and though I cared not much for the beast, this kind of dog having but little in him of wit or of affection, I received him for his master's sake. Well, walking abroad one Sunday evening, for the poor creature had been kept at home for some days by ill-weather, a hare chanced to cross my path, which the dog, almost before I could speak his name, had caught and killed. I thought that none had been offended in the matter, save, may be, my patron, and his pardon I had, when I confessed my offence to him. Master President looked mighty grave when I told my story, and said that the Court would consider it.

"After this breaks in another Commissioner with, 'We have been informed, Master Parson, that you were seen to stand by a bonfire some three years since.'

"' 'Tis true,' said I, 'I do remember hearing a great shouting in the village; I went forth and found three parts, as I should guess, of my parishioners assembled about a bonfire, but I had no other concern with it.'

"'Know you not,' said the Commissioner, 'that there is something superstitious and papistical about bonfires?'

"'This, at the least,' said I, 'was not papistical, for 'twas lighted on the fifth of November, and the people had burned—for so I heard, being myself too late to see it—the effigies of the Pope of Rome.'

"Then another Commissioner had his turn at me. 'We have heard that you suffer your children to play at cards for pins. Is this so?'

"'Am I bound,' said I, 'to answer any question to my own damage?' (For I was minded to have a little sport with them.)

"'We shall know how to interpret your silence,' says Master President.

"'Nay, then,' said I, 'if I must answer, I will. Children I have not, but one child only, a babe of six months only, who, I warrant you, so careful a mother has he—has never so much as had a pin in his fingers. And as for cards, he knows no more of such things than you yourself, Master Commissioner,' at which speech he reddened, having been not so long since, till he found his account in other ways, a noted card-player and gamester. To make a long matter short, they made out no case against me, for all that they brought every good-for-nothing fellow in the whole country side to give testimony against me. But I build not on this; I know right well that sentence was passed on me before ever I came into court."

And so indeed it turned out. Two days after my brother was summoned by the Commissioners to appear before them, and received sentence of deprivation, but to have as a *solatium* one fifth part of the proceeds of the living. This fifth part, I should here say, he never received, for the intruding minister alleged that he had some temporal means of his own, and that he had but one child (which was true, but scarce relevant, seeing that one child must eat as well as two), and that he himself could scarce get anything of tithes; which also I believe, for the farmers, who love not paying tithes at any time, were more especially set against them when they were to be received by the intruding minister.

My brother had angered some of the Commissioners by the freedom of his answering, and receiving warning that he had best be absent when the sentence was executed, went into hiding in a neighbour's house. The next day comes the constable, with some soldiers at his back, with a warrant to apprehend his person, and was greatly enraged when he found that the bird was flown. He and his fellows had at the best but little civility in them, and this they had done their best to banish by too plentiful cups, and indeed they behaved themselves more like savages than Christian men. They searched the house through for my brother, the constable running his sword two or three times through the bed from which my sister was but newly risen (for they came before seven o'clock in the forenoon), pretending that he might be there hidden. All the stores in the house they wasted most cruelly, spoiling that which they could not carry away. Indeed, they were bent on insult rather than plunder. Thus the troopers pulled the bridles off their horses, and whipped them round the garden to tread all under foot. After that they brake open the barn door and turned them into the sacks of corn to fill their bellies. Indeed, they would have burned the barn and all the hay and corn, but that the neighbours hindered them, fearing the fire for their own stack-yards. Nor would these suffer them to profane the church, which they would have done under cover of destroying papistical ornaments. Verily, I know not what these savages would have left undone but for the singular affection which the people had for my brother, who, indeed, had well discharged his priest's office among them since his coming into the parish, ministering without wearying both to their souls and bodies. Many of his brethren suffered worse things than he, especially in the cruelties that were wrought upon their wives and children, for these poor creatures were ofttimes driven out of their homes in the very depth and severity of winter, and forced to find such shelter as they could in barns and stables, and to live upon any broken victuals which they could beg or pick up, robbing the very swine. I know that the clergy which suffered such things were not blameless. Some had borne themselves haughtily and wantonly in the day of their prosperity, as lords of God's heritage rather than as shepherds of the flock; and some had

T

been careless livers, or worse, tippling at alehouses, or wandering about the country to bull-baiting, and village feasts, and church ales, where they brought the name of the Church into great disrepute. That these were rightly dispossessed I deny not. Such men are not worthy to labour in the garden of the Lord. But many pious men also suffered for nought else than that they kept that which they had vowed and promised. And when they who are now trodden under foot shall get the upper hand, as I doubt not they will—before we that are now young are come to middle-age—they, I fear me, will use the same cruelty. So does wrong beget wrong, and hatreds are stored up for the time to come that many generations shall not exhaust. I pray God that He may give my countrymen a better mind.

CHAPTER XXI.

OF MY ADVENTURES AT SEA.

It was but some three weeks after these things that my dear mother died. I would not lay her death to the door even of these cruel men, for 'tis certain that she had declined from the very beginning of her widowhood; but I cannot doubt that her end was hastened by grief and trouble. Notwithstanding, she passed away in great peace and comfort, having as lively a faith in the world to come—and in her meeting again with those whom in this world she had lost—as was ever seen in Christian woman. After her death, which took place in the house of the worthy neighbour who had given shelter to my brother's family at the first, my sister and her child took up their dwelling with John Vickers, which worthy man, whose kindness and truth I cannot sufficiently praise, most hospitably entertained her. Notwithstanding, she judged it best for her greater safety from molestation to lay aside her estate as a gentlewoman and to labour with her hands in the house and dairy. She told me afterwards that the good John was much troubled and distressed at her so humbling herself, and would doff his cap and show other courtesy to her which did contrast very strangely with her lowly dress, till by slow degrees and with much unwillingness he learnt to behave himself in a more suitable fashion.

Meanwhile, John Ellgood, having departed for his home, where his father much needed his presence, Master Blagrove and I set out for London, desiring there to settle some urgent affairs. He had some small property, for which he was desirous to make composition, and I was minded to do the same for my father's estate, if this could by any means be contrived. And here we met with an adventure which shall now be told.

We went on a certain afternoon to the Strand, purposing to visit my cousin Master Rushworth, of whom I have spoken before. We found him but half recovered of a sickness, but hearty in spirit, and as kind as ever he was.

Indeed, I marvelled a little at the praises which he and his wife heaped upon me. If they were to be believed, there had never been so well-behaved and admirable a boy. I did not remember myself to have possessed so many virtues, and, indeed, could bring to mind not a few reproofs which these good people had administered to me for sundry misdoings, ay, and prophecies that, unless I amended my ways, I should bring shame on all my kindred. Now this was all forgotten, and the good only remembered, a fault of memory, doubtless, but one which may easily be pardoned.

We stayed somewhat late with Master Rushworth over a flask of canary, which he would have replenished again and again had we suffered it. 'Twas ten of the clock, or thereabouts, when we set out for our lodging, which was in Westminster, and the street was almost deserted. We had scarce walked a hundred yards westward when there ran out upon us a company of fellows attired as sailors. I was unarmed save for a stout staff which I had in my hand, and my brother had not even so much; and we were also taken unawares, so that I had but time to strike one blow for my liberty. Even so, being very fleet of foot, I might have escaped, but could not in honour leave my companion who was an older man, and of a student's habit, which, as all know, is ill-fitted for bodily exercise. Hence the fellows laid hold upon us without much difficulty, and clapping handcuffs upon our hands, and gags in our mouths, had us at their mercy. They then carried us to a wherry, and so conveyed us to a ship which lay moored near the farther bank of the river, about half-a-mile below London Bridge. Being there arrived, and hoisted on to the deck, they took the gags from our mouths and lowered us into the hold. That we had company even in this place was easy to be told, for we heard the snoring of sleepers, and some round oaths also from someone, over whom, not knowing where we were, we stumbled; but how many they were and of what sort, we knew not, it being pitch dark. Thus we disposed ourselves as best we could, and, after the manner of St. Paul and his shipmates, "wished for the morning." When it was light, or as much light as the nature of the place permitted, and we could examine our company, we were not over-well pleased. There were some thirty in all, as villainous a set of jail-birds, the most of them, as ever was gathered together. Two or three, indeed, were as we afterwards learned, of a more honest sort, but the rest, it was manifest, were the very off-scouring of the prisons. Says one of them, a tall, stout fellow, that seemed to be a sort of captain among them :

"Come, friends, tell us how we came to have the honour of your company. Was it for lifting a purse, or breaking into a house, or cracking a man's skull ?"

Before I could answer he caught sight of my brother's clergyman's habit, and stirring with his foot one of the company that lay with his face to the wall, said :

"Parson, here is one of thy cloth ; up and bid him welcome to this meeting of good fellows."

The man raised himself, and turned his face to us, a more wretched countenance than ever I had seen before.

"I could not have believed," he said, "that there was anyone in the world so wretched as I ; yet, to judge from your habit, you are my fellow in misery. I have been sent down into this hell upon earth for no other offence save that I am a priest of the Church of England."

He then went on to tell us his history. He had, like thousands of others, been dispossessed of his living, and this with such circumstances of cruelty as cost him the life of his wife, who at the time of his expulsion was lain-in but a few days before of her first child. Afterwards, coming to London to see if he could make a livelihood by teaching, he had been kidnapped, as we had been.

"But what," I inquired of him, "will they do with us?"

"We are bound," said he, "for the plantations. 'Tis a monstrous thing that innocent men should be so dealt with. I do not say, for I would not be unjust for all my misery, that they who are in authority know of these doings. I judge that they do not. But they are careless; they make no inquiry. It matters not to them if there be some score of malignants the less to trouble them with their complaints, or to plot against them; so much the better. Hence the villains who carry on this business are emboldened to lay their hands upon us. Their occupation is to find labourers for the plantations in the Indies; and for each of these that they bring out they receive so many pounds sterling; how many I know not, but I take it that it is a considerable sum. They seek their recruits first in the jails. When these are overcrowded, and they never were crowded more than now, all England being overrun with disbanded soldiers, they find a plentiful supply. The magistrates, partly for gain, and partly for humanity's sake, hand over to them some that had else rotted in prison or stretched the hangman's rope, but if the tale be short, then they must make it up elsewhere; nor do they care at all how they come by their merchandise."

This was dismal hearing, and would have thrown us into despair had we had more leisure to think of it. As it was, we were fully occupied with the miseries of our present position. A more deplorable condition than ours it was scarce possible to conceive. For food we had biscuit, mouldy and full of weevils, and had it been more eatable, insufficient in quantity. Salted beef was also given to us, harder than ever I thought beef could be. Of water we had a sufficient quantity, a great barrel being set in the hold, over which one of the company, deputed to that office by his fellows, kept guard. This was the chief belightening of our lot. In another respect, also, its hardship was somewhat mitigated. At the first we suffered much from the hideousness of the oaths and blasphemy and foul lauguage of every kind which we heard from our companions. Having borne this for a day I resolved within myself to see whether I could not mend it. With this purpose in view I said to the captain, as I may call him, "I like not this talking. Will you please to change it?"

"Who are you," said he, "that pretend to order our behaviour? As you like it not, you can depart whither you will or can."

"Captain," said I, for so we called him, though he had never been more than a captain of thieves, "I would choose, if it may be, to be your friend rather than your foe. And you too, if you are wise, will choose the same. But I make this condition of peace, that there be no foul language or oaths, which in this narrow space, reach to ears for which doubtless they are not intended."

At this one of the captain's friends, a fellow of the sort that love always to play jackal to a lion, brake rudely in upon me with, "I know not whether your ears be daintier than other men's; but certainly they are longer."

I had resolved to have the matter out, if need were, with the captain himself, and did not doubt but that, being expert in manly exercises, and sound in health and wind, I should get the better of him. Nevertheless I would willingly have avoided such a conflict, knowing that it might leave ill-blood behind. So when this rude fellow interrupted me I saw an occasion of showing my strength which might serve my purpose better than giving the captain actual experience of it. Turning, therefore, upon the fellow I caught him by the collar of his coat, and held him out for some space of time at arm's length, which, as all who have tried such an action know, is no easy matter. When I put the man down, the captain stretched out his hand to me and said:

"You are right, good sir, we will be friends

rather than foes, and you shall have your way in this matter of talking. And hark ye, my friends," he said turning to the others; " he that speaks an ill word hereafter in this place must reckon with me."

This habit of foul speaking, like other ill habits, is not broken in a day, and the captain himself, who indeed had been wont to garnish his speech with as strange a variety of oaths as ever were heard from mortal tongue, was a frequent offender. But he was not, therefore, the less severe upon others; and before long there was a visible amendment. Then, again, we two and the two or three others of the better sort of whom I have already written, used our best endeavours to put something more edifying in the place of the thieves' stories with which these poor wretches were accustomed to entertain each other. They were, as may be readily supposed, wholly ignorant of all that it concerned them as Englishmen to know of the history of this realm; of gallant deeds that have been done by our countrymen on sea and land they had not so much as heard. Yet they listened eagerly enough to stories of such things, and were never wearied of hearing the tale of King Alfred fighting against the Danes, and of Harold, at whose defeat by the Conqueror they murmured loudly, and of the Black Prince at Cressy and Poictiers. With such narratives we kept them quiet and orderly, and my brother in particular, who had a most pleasant voice, gained such a mastery over them that when he proposed that they should say a few prayers with him both morning and evening, there was not a man to say him " Nay," and indeed at the end of a week's time he had a most respectful congregation.

How long we remained in this condition I cannot exactly say, for night and day were scarce to be distinguished in that place; but I consider it to have been as much as six weeks. That we were journeying south we knew from the heat, which had much increased so that the place was scarce endurable. We had indeed besought the men that brought us our provisions (which they lowered from above) that they would give us some more air, but had besought in vain, and were even thinking of getting by force what was then cruelly denied, when there happened that which made our schemes superfluous.

One night the wind began to rise (hitherto we had had extraordinary fine weather), and increased so much that we were tossed about in a most dangerous fashion. The seams of the ship also began to open, and to let in water, so that our condition became almost intolerable. The next day the hatches were opened, as they had never been opened before since our coming down on board, and a ladder was let down into the hold. "Come," cried one from above, "unless you would die like rats in a hole." We needed no second bidding, and indeed for the last two hours the water had been increasing upon us in most threatening fashion. No sooner had we reached the deck than we saw that the ship was lower in the water than promised well for her safety. And, indeed, what with the lowering sky and the waves, that were like mountains on every side of us, the prospect was gloomy, and it seemed that we had recovered our liberty only that we might perish. Nevertheless, we thought it better to die in the open air and in the light, even as

Ajax the Greater prays to Jupiter, "Slay me, so it be in the light." Says the man that had let down the ladder, whom we now found to be the mate, "Come, my friends, if you would see land again; set your hands to the pumps." This we did with a good will and with such strength as was still left us by our imprisonment and scanty diet. For a time we lost rather than gained, and it seemed as if our days were numbered; but as it grew towards evening, the wind abated and the sea fell, so that it brake not over the ship as before. By good fortune also the carpenter discovered the principal leak and repaired it, so that about an hour after sunset, by which time indeed we were well nigh spent with labour, we had respite from pumping, and ate the supper which the mate had caused to be prepared for us. 'Twas no very luxurious banquet, but 'twas royal fare to us, and we feasted with as good an appetite as ever men had in this world. While we sat at meal the mate told us what had happened.

"We had, you must know," he said, "but one boat, and that would contain but two parts of the crew. Well, when it appeared this morning that the ship could hardly swim much longer, and there seemed no sign of the weather abating, the captain contrived that the carpenter and I and three more of us should go below, if we might chance to find any of the leaks. And while we were gone, he and the others lowered the boat, which was already fitted and provisioned, and so departed. A villain I knew him to be, but had not thought him capable of such wickedness. But I reckon that he has made a mistake, for all his cunning. I had ten times sooner be here, things being as they are, than in the boat with him."

And indeed the mate was right, for the captain and the rest of the crew were never heard of more.

The next day the sea was as calm as though it were a pond, and the sky without a cloud. I asked the mate whereabouts, in his judgment, we were. "God only knows," he said. "The Captain took the reckoning, and he has the instruments with him, for I cannot find them. But I remember him to have said the day before the storm that we were about four hundred miles from our journey's end. But I reckon that we must now be more than that, the wind for the last day having blown very strongly from the west."

"What then," said I, "would you have us do?"

"I think that we had best sail westward, for, even if we have been driven back two hundred miles or more, the nearest land must still lie in that quarter. We will rig up a jury mast" (for both the ship's masts had been lost in the storm), "and sail as best we may; but I must confess that my great hope is in falling in with some ship that may help us."

But we were not yet past all our troubles. That rascal, whom I have called the "captain," and some of his fellows, having found where the spirits were kept, brake open the place, and helped themselves to the liquor. Inflamed by drinking, they conceived the plan (first hatched, I believe, in the brain of the fellow with whom I had the passage of arms before described) of making themselves masters of the ship and taking to the trade of buccaneers or pirates, between whom, I take it, there is no great distinction. Accordingly they seize the mate in his bed, to which, after I know not how many days' toil and watching, he had betaken himself for a few hours' rest, bring over the remainder of the crew to their side by threats and promises, and clap those of the company whom they had no hope of persuading into the hold again.

I must confess that at this ill turn of fortune I began to despair, but found comfort where I had least expected it. For now the poor parson, of whose doleful countenance I have before written, plays the part of a St. Paul.

"Be of good cheer," says he, "for I am persuaded that He who has helped us so far will not now desert us. I was as downcast as you now are; and God sent you to cheer me up. Let me do the same office now for you, for I have learnt that to despair is nothing less than a sin against God."

And sure enough the good man was in the right. We had not been in our prison more than three or four hours when we overheard a loud noise as of talking and tramping of feet overhead, and not long after, to our great joy, saw the hatches thrown open, and were released from our duress. What had happened may be briefly told.

The mutineers had scarce made themselves masters of the ship when there hove in sight a strange sail, which, by great good fortune, or, I should rather say, by God's kind providence, was a Dutch man-of-war. She was heading right for us, and the villains, having but a poor pretence of mast and sail, had no chance of escape. The Dutchman seeing a vessel in distress, as was evident from our appearance, sends one of his officers on board. The villains speak him fair, and tell a plausible tale, which, but for the carpenter, might have deceived him. But the carpenter, who had given in to the mutineers only for fear of his life, whispers in the officer's ear that he had best inquire further. And so the whole truth comes out.

The mutineers, having some bold fellows among them, would, I doubt not, have made a fight for the mastery, but were so ill-armed that they durst not venture. To make my story short, when the Dutch captain came on board and had heard how matters stood, he came to this conclusion.

"The ship, which was but a rotten craft before, and is now damaged by the storm beyond repair, I shall take leave to scuttle. As for the villains they would but meet with their proper deserts were I to leave them to sink with her, or hang them from my yard-arm. But I care not to have their blood upon my soul. Yet I should be doing but an ill-turn to mankind were I to take them back to Europe. It seems to me, therefore, the best course to leave them on some uninhabited island, of which there is more than one in these seas, where they may earn their bread by tilling the soil, or, if it please them better, cut each other's throats. As for you, gentlemen, I shall be happy to give you a passage back to Holland, to which country I am now bound."

And this he did. Never was a more courteous host, or guests who were better pleased with their entertainment. I had much talk with the good man during the voyage, which, the wind being often light and baffling, occupied near upon two months, and among other things related to him the story of my life. And this, by his counsel, I have now written down.

EPILOGUE.

ROTTERDAM, May 1st, 1660.

'TIS about eleven years since I wrote in this book of how I had been with the King at Oxford, and of other things which grew out of the same. And now, if anyone should desire to know how I and others of whom mention has been made in this writing have since fared, I will in a very few words here set it forth.

Being brought to Holland after my escape from the kidnappers, as related in the chapter last written, and seeking some means of earning my bread, I chanced to meet with a certain merchant of Rotterdam, Richard Daunt by name, who, having satisfied himself that I was a man of decent conversation and sufficient scholarship, would have me come to him as a tutor to his sons. "And you shall find," he said, "others of our nation at Rotterdam, who will gladly put their children in your charge."

To this I was willing enough to hearken, nor have I ever repented that I did so, having found in Master Daunt and his fellows at Rotterdam, as good friends as a man could desire to have.

About a year after my going to Rotterdam, the charge of minister to the congregation of English merchants in that city fell vacant, by the cession of Master Richard Chalfont, some time Fellow of Lincoln College, by whose good word, many of the congregation also favouring, I had from the Committee the promise of the succession, if only I could obtain Holy Orders. This agreed well with what had always been my desire, and I determined to seek Orders from some Bishop in England, if only one could be found able and willing to give them; for this, in the distress of the times, could not be with certainty counted upon. I knew of none in England from whom I could get better information and advice than Master Ellgood. To him, therefore, I resolved to resort, not, it will readily be believed without the thought present in my mind of seeing again my dear Cicely; for it had been long understood that we were to be married so soon as I had reasonable prospect of maintaining a wife. Master Ellgood behaved himself most friendly to me. When I asked him about the obtaining of Orders, he said:

" 'Tis not impossible. My Lord of Oxford, or, to speak more agreeably with the spirit of the times, Dr. Robert Skinner, has licence to give them, or, I should rather say, having friends among them that are in power, is winked at in so doing."

Hearing this, I expounded to the good man my hopes and plans, which he encouraged, knowing that I had for a long time cherished this design.

"The charge at Rotterdam," said I, "is worth eighty pounds by the year; and I can add as much more by the teaching of English boys in that city, for which employment I shall have ample time. If then I can satisfy the bishop of my fitness (of which I have a good hope), after having received Orders from him, I will ask you to give me your daughter Cicely in marriage."

"I like not," said he, "that a priest should marry, nor can I give my consent that he should marry a daughter of mine."

'Twas as if a thunderbolt had fallen upon me when I heard him say these words. Cicely, too, for she was present at our conference, grew suddenly pale.

"Nay, my good sir," I said, "how can that be? Does not St. Paul say that a bishop should be 'the husband of one wife'?"

"I am not so careless a student of holy Scripture," answered he, "as to have overlooked that text. Yet, having studied Christian antiquity with all the diligence that I could use, I could never find one instance in which a priest (to which I take the word 'bishop' to be here equal) has contracted matrimony. But that married men have been ordained priests and deacons I know full well, and this, which indeed is the custom of the Greek Church, I take to be the apostle's meaning. So, then, if you are willing to marry my daughter before ordination, I refuse not my consent, but rather give it, and my blessing with it, most willingly."

At this, which the good man said not without a certain twinkle in his eye, Cicely, if she had been pale before, grew red; but was not so displeased but that when I reached out my hand to hers and took it she suffered it to remain.

The next day I set out for Launton, where Dr. Skinner had his charge, in which, indeed, he had not been disturbed. With him I sojourned three days, and, after being closely examined in my knowledge of Scripture and other matters with which a clergyman should have some acquaintance, received from him a promise, which he put in writing for the satisfaction of Master Ellgood, that he would presently admit me both to deacon's and priest's orders.

In two weeks time after my return from the bishop my sweet Cicely and I were married, first by a neighbouring magistrate (for so marriages were performed at that time), and after by one of the dispossessed clergy, that was chaplain to one of the gentry in those parts, Master Ellgood saying that he was still, however worthy, under ecclesiastical censure, and could perform no spiritual function. And again, in two weeks more I was ordained deacon by Dr. Skinner, and, being of full age, because it would not be convenient for me to come again to England, priest on the day following. I thank my God that he gave me His two best gifts, a good calling in life, and a good helpmeet. Verily they are gifts of which I have not repented me for a moment, though I must confess that I am scarce worthy of them.

My Cicely's father has lived with us since our marriage, busying himself with books and with good works. John Ellgood has risen to a high place in the Stadtholder's service.

My brother-in-law has for the last ten years been chaplain to my Lord Brandon, and has found under his protection both safety and comfort.

It is now, I hear, a settled thing that monarchy shall be restored in England. I could wish that there were a better report of the new King. That he will avoid his father's faults, I doubt not, for 'tis his settled resolve, as has often been heard from his mouth, to die King of England, and he will not imperil his crown by obstinacy or self-will. But he is lacking in his father's best virtues, and 'tis much to be doubted whether England will get much advantage from his coming back. But God can overrule all things for good, and 'twere lack of faith to doubt that He will.

THE END.

BY THE SAME AUTHOR.

THE CHANTRY PRIEST OF BARNET: A
Tale of the Two Roses. With Coloured Illustrations. Price 5s.

STORIES FROM HOMER. With Coloured Illustrations. *Sixteenth Thousand.* Price 5s., cloth.

STORIES FROM VIRGIL. With Coloured Illustrations. *Twelfth Thousand.* Price 5s., cloth.

STORIES FROM THE GREEK TRAGEDIANS.
With Coloured Illustrations. *Eighth Thousand.* Price 5s., cloth.

STORIES OF THE EAST FROM HERODOTUS. With Coloured Illustra'ions. *Seventh Thousand.* Price 5s., cloth.

THE STORY OF THE PERSIAN WAR FROM HERODOTUS. With Coloured Illustrations. *Fourth Thousand.* Price 5s., cloth.

STORIES FROM LIVY. With Coloured Illustrations. *Fourth Thousand.* Price 5s., cloth.

ROMAN LIFE IN THE DAYS OF CICERO.
With Coloured Illustrations. *Fourth Thousand.* Price 5s., cloth.

THE STORY OF THE LAST DAYS OF JERUSALEM FROM JOSEPHUS. With Coloured Illustrations. *Fourth Thousand.* Price 3s. 6d., cloth.

A TRAVELLER'S TRUE TALE FROM LUCIAN. With Coloured Illustrations. *Third Thousand.* Price 3s. 6d., cloth.

HEROES AND KINGS. Stories from the Greek.
Price 1s. 6d., cloth.

SEELEY & CO., ESSEX STREET, STRAND.

RECENTLY PUBLISHED.

BORDER LANCES: A Romance of the Northern Marches. By the Author of "Belt and Spur." With Coloured Illustrations. Price 5s., cloth.

STORIES OF THE ITALIAN PAINTERS FROM VASARI. With Coloured Illustrations. Price 5s., cloth.

BELT AND SPUR. Stories of the Knights of Old. *Fourth Thousand.* With Sixteen Illuminations. Price 5s., cloth.

THE CITY IN THE SEA. Stories of the Old Venetians. By the Author of "Belt and Spur." With Coloured Illustrations. Price 5s., cloth.

HORACE WALPOLE AND HIS WORLD. Select passages from his Letters. With Eight copper-plates after Sir Joshua Reynolds and Sir Thomas Lawrence. Price 6s., cloth. Also a Large-paper Edition, with Proofs of the Plates. Price 12s. 6d.

SUN, MOON, AND STARS. A Book on Astronomy for Beginners. By A. GIBERNE. With Coloured Illustrations. *Eleventh Thousand.* Price 5s., cloth.

THE WORLD'S FOUNDATIONS. Geology for Beginners. By A. GIBERNE. With Illustrations. *Third Thousand.* Price 5s., cloth.

AMONG THE STARS. Wonderful Things in the Sky. Astronomy for Children. With Illustrations. Price 5s., cloth.

SINTRAM AND HIS COMPANIONS. By DE LA MOTTE FOUQUE. A New Translation. With numerous Illustrations by Heywood Sumner. Price 5s., cloth.

THE PHARAOHS AND THEIR LAND: Scenes of Old Egyptian Life and History. By E. BERKLEY. With Coloured Illustrations. Price 5s., cloth.

SEELEY & CO., ESSEX STREET, STRAND.

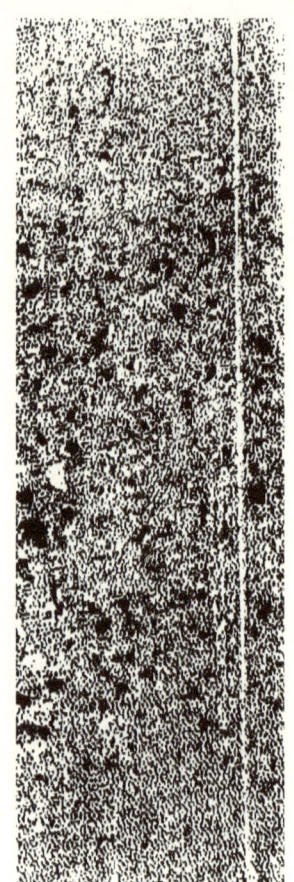

www.ingramcontent.com/pod-product-compliance
Lightning Source LLC
Chambersburg PA
CBHW030324240426
43673CB00040B/1268